Serverless Single Page Apps

Fast, Scalable, and Available

Ben Rady

The Pragmatic Bookshelf

Raleigh, North Carolina

Many of the designations used by manufacturers and sellers to distinguish their products are claimed as trademarks. Where those designations appear in this book, and The Pragmatic Programmers, LLC was aware of a trademark claim, the designations have been printed in initial capital letters or in all capitals. The Pragmatic Starter Kit, The Pragmatic Programmer, Pragmatic Programming, Pragmatic Bookshelf, PragProg and the linking *g* device are trademarks of The Pragmatic Programmers, LLC.

Every precaution was taken in the preparation of this book. However, the publisher assumes no responsibility for errors or omissions, or for damages that may result from the use of information (including program listings) contained herein.

Our Pragmatic books, screencasts, and audio books can help you and your team create better software and have more fun. Visit us at *https://pragprog.com*.

The team that produced this book includes:

Jacquelyn Carter (editor)
Potomac Indexing, LLC (index)
Nicole Abramowitz, Liz Welch (copyedit)
Gilson Graphics (layout)
Janet Furlow (producer)

For sales, volume licensing, and support, please contact *support@pragprog.com*.

For international rights, please contact *rights@pragprog.com*.

Printed in the United States of America.
ISBN-13: 978-1-68050-149-0
Printed on acid-free paper.
Book version: P1.0—June 2016

To my wife Jenny, who gives me strength;
My daughter Katherine, for her kindness;
And my son Will, who'll save the world

Contents

Acknowledgments

Thanks to Jackie Carter, my editor, as well as Dave, Andy, and everyone else at The Pragmatic Bookshelf for their time, support, and energy. I could not have created this book without you.

Thanks to all my technical reviewers, including Alex Disney, Clinton Begin, Daniel Hinojosa, David Rupp, Jake McCrary, James Ross, Jeff Sacks, Joshua Graham, Lucas Ward, Rene Duquesnoy, Rob Churchwell, Ryan Brown, and Sebastian Krueger.

Thanks to everyone at Amazon who helped me validate the ideas in this book, including Tim Wagner, Bob Kinney, Tim Hunt, and Will Gaul.

Also, thanks to everyone who provided other feedback during the beta, either personally, via the errata page, on the forums, or on Github.com, including Bill Caputo, Christopher Brackert, Christopher Moeller, Dennis Burke, Ezequiel Rangel, Fred Daoud, Hal Wine, Jerry Tang, Ron Campbell, and Timm Knape.

Thank you all for helping me create this book! Your feedback was invaluable to me, and I truly appreciate your time and attention.

Introduction

After years of building single page web applications and wishing that I could break free of the constraints imposed by application servers, my wish has come true. Amazon (and, increasingly, other companies) have developed technologies that make it possible to use a *serverless* approach that removes a lot of the risks and costs of building and scaling web applications. This idea is so compelling and so transformative that I had to write a book about it.

I wrote this book for the people I know in my life who want to build something on the web. Some have an app they want to build—something they think will be the next big thing. Some are just starting out in web development and have never built any kind of app—world-changing or otherwise. And some are experienced web developers who've built dozens of Model-View-Controller based web apps with Java, Ruby on Rails, or Node.js. With the emergence of this new technology, I want to share what I've learned about it, in the hopes that someone out there will use it to build something great.

In this introductory chapter, you'll get an idea of what to expect from this book and what you can do to get the most out of it.

Guiding Principles

I wrote this book with a few guiding principles in mind. The purpose of these principles is to focus the scope of the book and make it accessible and relevant to you, the reader. I've listed these principles here to give you some insight into how I've written this book and to help you better understand the context of the material you're about to read.

Some of these principles may be potentially controversial. Some of them even run counter to popular thinking about how to build web applications. However, these principles will help you understand this topic in depth. It's better to be controversial than try to be everything to everybody.

Use Web Standards and Familiar Tools

In this book, you'll use a small, curated set of tools to build a single page web application. At certain points in the book, you'll create functionality that other tools already provide—tools that I've intentionally not included in the app. You might wonder why we're not using those tools if they provide needed functionality.

Reading a book of this sort is fundamentally an act of learning. When learning, it's helpful to work with familiar tools. Otherwise, you wind up spending more time learning about the tools than learning the technique. I didn't want the choice of a framework or library to be a distraction. This book is about serverless web applications, not frameworks or libraries. To remain agnostic, we'll instead lean on tools that are familiar to web developers (like jQuery), web standards, and the web services that make a serverless design possible.

 This book is about web services, not web frameworks.

It's possible that after reading this book, you'll reach for a client-side web framework, such as React or Angular, to build your own web apps. These tools have gained a lot of traction in the web development community in the last few years, and I expect we'll see many successful projects that use them. Everything you'll learn in this book is compatible with anything you'll want to do with these frameworks. They are complementary, not contradictory.

Use Functional JavaScript

In this book, you won't be creating any classes in JavaScript. Creating class hierarchies to solve problems can make sense in languages with rich, object-oriented type systems, but JavaScript isn't one of those languages. Instead, we'll use a functional style that's easier to understand.

This means you won't get caught up in scoping issues with the this keyword. You'll avoid prototypes and inheritance altogether. You won't use the new keyword paired with specially designed functions to create objects; instead, you'll create them using the object literal: {}.

You can decide for yourself if this is a style you want to adopt. While some real, tangible benefits to this approach exist, at the end of the day, many software design decisions come down to preference and style. Code, after all, should be written for humans first and computers second. As long as it works, it doesn't matter to the computer what the code looks like.

Avoid Yaks

When working on a project, my goal is always this: deliver incremental improvement steadily over time, in any direction the environment demands, for as long as is needed. Meeting this goal means avoiding anything that causes my rate of delivery to grind to a halt, like a lot of *yak shaving*.

If you're not familiar with the term *yak shaving*, imagine you want to buy a sweater as a gift for a friend. You go to the store only to discover it has no sweaters to sell. Fortunately, another customer there knows of a great tailor down the street who might be able to make you one. So you head to the tailor, who has a wonderful sweater pattern and a machine that can knit it, but the yarn supplier hasn't made a delivery today. So you head to the supplier...

And this continues on and on until you find yourself in a field in western Tibet, shaving a yak to spin yarn. "How did I get here?" you might ask yourself. "All I wanted was a sweater." When a chain of seemingly related and necessary tasks distracts you from your real goal, you're yak shaving. Thankfully, the cure for yak shaving is often simply to realize that you're yak shaving and buy a hat instead.

I want to keep you from shaving yaks while reading this book. That's why I use a prepared workspace and a minimal set of tools. You should spend your time learning, not installing, configuring, and troubleshooting.

Move Faster with Tests

Have you ever been scared to change a bit of code? Maybe you were unsure about what it was supposed to do or why it was supposed to do it. "First, do no harm" applies to programmers as well as doctors. Situations like this can make you feel like you're stuck.

Imagine if you had a trusted colleague—an expert in that system—sitting next to you as you made those changes. If you introduced any bug into the system, you would be interrupted with a clear and concise explanation of why this change would be a Bad Idea. If you had this trusted colleague, would you have been stuck then?

Uncertainty slows us down and limits the scope of our solutions. To build software quickly, you must work with *confidence*. To get that confidence, you can create your own automated expert—something that knows every detail of the system, how it works, and why it works like it does. This expert can live alongside the system, changing as it changes, one a reflection of the other. You can create this expert with a suite of tests that is fast enough to run continuously—hundreds of tests per second—after every change you make to the code.

Once you have a suite of tests in place, new options open up to you. When you no longer fear change, you can design the application as you go, rather than trying to get it "right" from the start. This means you can quickly adapt to the world as it changes, instead of trying to predict what you'll need and what you won't. You can base decisions on current information instead of speculation, and the application will be as simple as it can be for now.

In this book, you'll use a technique called *test-driven development (TDD)* to write both the application and its tests. Learning to build software with tests is a skill, and you have to practice it if you want to reap the benefits. My goal in including TDD in this book is not only to show you how to test specific kinds of behavior in web apps, but also to demonstrate how easy it is to test a typical web application, if you know how to do it.

When practicing TDD, you work in a three-step cycle, usually expressed as Red-Green-Refactor. First, you write a test that checks for behavior that the program doesn't yet have. If the test fails the way you expect, then you can be confident that it is testing the behavior you want to add to the app. Now the tests are *Red*. Once you have a failing test, add the simplest code you can to make the test pass...usually a few lines. Now the tests are *Green*.

After you've added some behavior to the app using a test, it's time to take a step back and look at the bigger picture. Have you introduced some duplicate code with the implementation? Do all the variables and functions have descriptive and accurate names? Is there a simpler approach that you missed? Now is the time to think about these things and *Refactor*. Refactoring is changing code without changing its behavior. The tests you've written will tell you whether or not you've changed the behavior, so it's important to refactor only when they're passing. Using this as your safety net, you can clean up any issues with the code before moving on to the next test.

The more you practice TDD, the faster you'll go, and the more value you'll get from it. By repeating this Red-Green-Refactor process over and over, you'll learn how to incrementally build an application that is well designed and well tested. This will not only give you confidence that your software works, but will also make it easier for you to change it over time.

Learn by Doing

This book is a tutorial, so you'll learn by doing. Throughout this book, you'll build a serverless single page web application as a running example. The purpose of this tutorial is to explain the concepts of serverless architecture in a concrete way. Because the result of this tutorial is a working application,[1] you can have confidence that the techniques in this book work as advertised.

Taking this approach means I can't go into as much depth as I might like without turning the book into a 400-page tome. For that reason, I've added a "Next Steps" section to every chapter to give you some additional topics to dig into if you want a little more.

Start with a Prepared Workspace

To get you up and running quickly, I've provided a *prepared workspace.* It includes everything you need to get started and shouldn't take long to set up. Imagine you were painting a work of art; I've gathered the paint, the easel, and the canvas for you. All that's left for you to do is create.

To use this prepared workspace, you'll need a computer with a Bash-compatible shell to use the scripts and utilities included. This can be OS X, any *nix flavor, or FreeBSD. You can probably get by with Windows if you have Cygwin installed. You'll also need a web browser with a developer console. I used Google Chrome for most of the examples in this book, but Firefox provides similar functionality in most cases.

How to Read This Book

You can read a book in many ways, not just the obvious one. Which approach you should take with this book depends on what you want to achieve. Here, you'll find some common reasons for reading a book like this, and my recommendation for how to use this book to best achieve those goals.

Goal #1: Understand Serverless vs. Traditional Single Page Apps

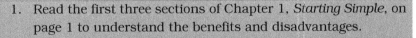

What to Do

1. Read the first three sections of Chapter 1, *Starting Simple*, on page 1 to understand the benefits and disadvantages.

2. Skim through the remainder of Chapter 1, as well as Chapters 2 and 3.

3. Read through Chapters 4–8, working along with the tutorial where possible.

---

1. http://learnjs.benrady.com

If you're an experienced web developer who has built single page web apps before, and you want to learn more about serverless web applications, you probably don't need all the material in the first three chapters. These chapters show a (more or less) vanilla.js approach to building single page web applications. The intent here is to demonstrate the fundamental components of a single page web app. I'm trying to define what parts are essential, and offer some basic implementations to act as a reference. If you don't write a lot of tests for your web apps, you can work through some of the testing examples in Chapter 2 to pick up some new skills.

After reading the first three sections in the first chapter, you'll want to concentrate your attention on Chapters 4–8. I do suggest that you build a simple web application, or at least a skeleton of one, so that you can try out the techniques in the later chapters for yourself. You can learn a lot through experimentation.

Goal #2: Build Your First Single Page App

What to Do
1. Read any of the following necessary supporting material before getting started.
2. Work through all the chapters, and, if necessary, the appendices.

If you're building a web application for the first time, you'll want to read the entire book, possibly cover to cover. In addition, you'll want to make sure you're up to speed on basic web technologies, including HTML, Cascading Style Sheets (CSS), and JavaScript. Check out the *Free Resources* here to get going. Once you understand these topics, dive into the book.

Free Resources

Learn to Code HTML & CSS [How14] by Shay Howe[a]

Eloquent JavaScript [Hav14] by Marijn Haverbeke[b]

---

a.   http://learn.shayhowe.com/html-css/
b.   http://eloquentjavascript.net/

Goal #3: Build a Serverless App Using Your Favorite Web Framework

What to Do

1. Work through Chapter 1.

2. Replicate the tests and functionality in Chapters 2 and 3 using your favorite web framework.

3. Work through Chapters 4–8.

As I've already mentioned, I didn't want this book to focus on web frameworks, but you can certainly use them to build serverless single page apps. If you're familiar with the basic elements of a single page app, and you rely on a client-side web framework to provide those for you, you can easily reproduce the functionality we create in Chapters 2 and 3 using that framework. Once you have that functionality in place, you should be able to follow along with the rest of the tutorial, adapting where necessary to meet the expectations of your framework of choice.

Goal #4: Create a Minimum Viable Product (MVP)

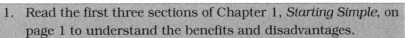

What to Do

1. Read the first three sections of Chapter 1, *Starting Simple*, on page 1 to understand the benefits and disadvantages.

2. Read *Costs of the Cloud*, on page 169 to understand the costs of building an MVP this way.

3. If the approach seems reasonable, read all the remaining chapters (and the appendices, if necessary).

4. Use the prepared workspace as a starting point to build your MVP.

When starting a new product or business, your first and most important challenge is to figure out what the market wants to buy and what it's willing to pay. Many people refer to this as *product/market fit*, and finding it is the key to building a successful product or service.

One effective way to find a product/market fit is to simply build a product and try to sell it. Validating both the demand in the market and your ability to connect with those customers via a sales or marketing channel is a critical hurdle that you should overcome as soon as possible. Of course, building a complete application for this purpose can take much more time and money than what you have available, so an alternative is to build a minimum viable product that demonstrates the product's core value.

Serverless single page apps are a great way to try a new idea, explore a potential new market, or create a minimum viable product. Building these kinds of applications in lieu of traditional web apps or native apps means you can get to your customers faster. You can build an initial version in only hours and deploy it in seconds. These apps can be updated instantly, are easily split tested, and can provide detailed usage metrics that help you understand what your customers want.

In addition to being inexpensive to run, quick to build, and almost universally accessible by users, serverless single page apps can scale "without limits" (as Amazon likes to say), so that if your product taps into a strong demand in the marketplace, you can meet that demand and retain the customers you acquire.

Online Resources

You can find the apps and examples shown in this book at The Pragmatic Bookshelf website for this book.[2] You'll also find the community forum and the errata-submission form, where you can report problems with the text or make suggestions for future versions.

You can find the prepared workspace under my account (benrady) at Github.com.[3] If you don't have one already, create an account and fork the repository to get started. For more detailed instructions on how to do this, see *Using Your Workspace*, on page 8.

Ben Rady
benrady@gmail.com
June 2016

---

2.   https://pragprog.com/book/brapps/serverless-page-apps
3.   https://github.com/benrady/learnjs

CHAPTER 1

Starting Simple

If you've ever thought, "There should be an app for that" and wondered who could build it for you, I have good news. We found someone. It's you.

Web applications can be powerful, efficient, and scalable, but they don't need to be complicated. Their simplicity is one of their great strengths, and you can use that strength to realize your own ideas and build your own solutions. Once you understand how all the pieces fit together, you'll be able to create the apps you want to see in the world.

This book is a practical tutorial that will demonstrate a *serverless* approach to building web applications. Using this approach, you can ignore most of the operational concerns and costs that come from running your own servers. You'll be able to focus time and attention on building the apps you want and let someone else worry about the headaches of provisioning, configuring, upgrading, and scaling servers to meet your needs as they grow. You won't achieve these gains in efficiency by adding multiple layers of web frameworks, generated code, or copy-and-paste templates. As we move through this tutorial together, you'll see how to deliver better applications by *removing* code and eliminating the middle-tier layers found in a traditional web application.

To start this tutorial quickly, we'll use a prepared workspace loaded with everything you'll need to build a complete web app. First, we'll build a *single page web app*, moving logic normally found in the server down into a web client built with JavaScript, HTML, and CSS. We'll rely primarily on web standards and dig deeply into the essential functions of single page web apps, building them up from scratch to both learn how they work and ensure the design fits the needs of our app. When our needs can't be met by web standards alone, we'll use jQuery to fill in the gaps. We'll make our single page app testable by building it incrementally, using a *Test First* approach.

To eliminate middle-tier costs and ensure our app scales into the millions of users, we'll use Amazon Web Services (AWS) to build a serverless back end. You'll see how to replace the servers, databases, and load balancers found in a traditional web application architecture with highly available and scalable cloud-based web services that are cheaper and easier to maintain. We'll look at some of the security issues you'll be faced with when building these kinds of applications, and we'll survey other technologies and tools you may want to use as your apps grow.

With this book, I hope to open new possibilities. Applications that previously were too expensive and time consuming to be worthwhile may become something you can finish in a day or two. As technology improves and expands your capabilities, more of your dreams will come into reach. As your understanding of these technologies grows, you'll begin to see new paths that lead you to goals you previously thought were too difficult to achieve. By the end of this journey, you'll have the skills you need to turn your ideas into reality.

Serverless Web Applications

Traditional web applications assume that the server is an essential part of the system. While sometimes fronted by a load balancer and/or dedicated web server, the *application server* does most of the heavy lifting. It performs all the essential functions of the app, including storing the user's data, issuing security credentials, and controlling navigation. The web portion of the web app is often just there to provide an interface to the back end, although some of the responsibility for controlling navigation rests there too. Many people call this traditional approach an *n-tier architecture*, where the browser, the application server, and one or more back-end services make up the tiers in the system.

With a serverless approach, you can remove all these tiers in favor of something more direct. Instead of treating the web client as the interface to the application server, you can move the application logic into the browser by building a single page web application. This means you can serve your application from a simple static web host—nothing more than a delivery mechanism for the app—while the browser acts as an application container. As you can see here, the result is a design that removes the middlemen from traditional web application architectures and allows the browser to directly connect to any services that it needs.

By using OAuth 2.0 identity providers such as Facebook, Google, and Twitter, you can create user identities without storing passwords. To store data, you can connect to services like Amazon DynamoDB right from the browser. Any

N-Tier Design

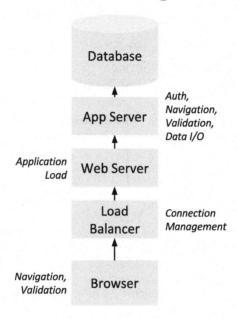

function that can't be performed in the browser can be handled by an Amazon Lambda microservice or other specialized web service. In addition to simplifying the architecture, making this transition to a web service back end lets you take advantage of the availability and scalability inherent in these services.

You might wonder what's changed to make this approach possible. Why is it only now that middle-tier application servers have become optional in a web application? The answer is, starting in 2015, cloud service providers such as Amazon began to provide APIs to their services to make this approach not only feasible, but a well-supported use case of their tools and infrastructure.

By building a single page web app based on web standards, rather than server-side web frameworks, we can quickly adopt these emerging technologies. For example, we don't have to tie our application's data model to any object hierarchy or data synchronization mechanism. That makes it easy to integrate with these kinds of services. Since we're starting from the foundations of the web, we don't have to fight against preconceptions of how a web application should be built, and we can create an application that is perfectly suited to the new technologies now available to us.

Serverless Design

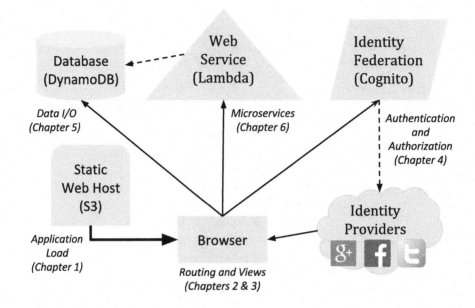

Benefits of a Serverless Design

If you're looking for a way to quickly build a low-cost web application, a serverless web app might be the solution. Rather than spending your time and energy on understanding all the different layers of a typical web application stack, this approach lets you focus on delivering features to your users while letting someone else worry about the headaches of runtime operations and scalability. Let's take a look at some of these benefits in depth, so that you can make an informed decision about whether this approach is right for your next project.

No More Servers

One of the most obvious benefits of a serverless design is that you don't have servers (physical or virtual) to maintain. You don't have to worry about applying security patches, monitoring CPU or memory use, rolling log files, running out of disk space, or any of the other operational issues that come up when maintaining your own servers. As with most Platform as a Service (PaaS) approaches, a serverless web application keeps you focused on your app, not worried about your infrastructure.

Easy to Scale

Another enormous benefit of this design is that it lets you rely on cloud service providers to scale your application. Rather than trying to keep data consistent between load-balanced application servers as you scale them horizontally, you can connect directly to web services that have already solved this problem. This means whether your application has just a handful of users, a few hundred, or a few hundred thousand, you can make sure it works flawlessly simply by changing a few settings in the Amazon Web Services console.

Highly Available

High availability also becomes much easier to achieve with this design. You no longer have to bring down your application server in order to upgrade it, or build out the infrastructure needed to perform a "hot" deploy. There are no service restarts to coordinate or deployment packages to copy from server to server. Best of all, you have the well-trained staff at Amazon watching your infrastructure 24/7, ready and able to respond if a problem arises.

Low Cost

The costs of these services can also be very low. Using a serverless approach and Amazon's Free Tier, you can often run your application for pennies a month. Once you exceed the free tier, costs often scale linearly (at worst) with the number of users you add. The application we'll build in this tutorial scales up to one million users for less than the cost of a cup of coffee per day.

(Micro)Service Friendly

This approach easily accommodates microservices and other service-oriented architectures. You can introduce specialty services into the system to perform custom authentication, validation, or asynchronous data processing. You can even reintroduce application servers, if you find a reason to do so, and gradually refactor your application to start using it. In contrast, if you start with a middle tier that holds all of the security credentials, it can be difficult to transition to web services that require authentication. The application server may not be able to manage identity at an application level like a serverless app can.

Less Code

With a traditional web application, operations that need to be performed in both the web client and the server, like navigation, result in duplicated code. Sometimes, this duplication is not immediately apparent, especially if the server is written in a different language. Since the application logic moves into the client with a serverless app, it becomes much easier to ensure that there's no duplication anywhere in your app. Unifying the application logic in one place (and one language) helps resolve this problem.

This approach can also be much easier to build and troubleshoot, because there are simply fewer actors in the system. Web applications are inherently distributed; that is, they pass messages (usually in the form of requests and responses) between nodes in a network and are limited in how they can do this, as described in the CAP theorem.[1]

Some apps are more distributed than others, and the more distributed your system, the harder it can be to troubleshoot. Removing tiers from your application can make it less distributed. In the simple case, if a client needs to fetch data from a database, they connect directly to the database rather than going through a middle tier. This means fewer network nodes in the system, which means fewer places to look if things go wrong.

As you can see, you might want to build a serverless app for a lot of reasons. As we move through this tutorial, you'll be able to see firsthand why this approach can be so powerful. With these benefits in mind, let's now take a look at some of the limitations of a serverless app.

Serverless Design Limitations

While a serverless architecture has many benefits, it isn't suited to every type of application. You have to accept a number of limitations in order to get the benefits of this design, and if your application can't work with those limitations, then this isn't the right approach. Let's take a look at some of those limits before we get started building our app.

Vendor Lock-In

The first and most significant limitation of this design is that you must use web services that support an identity provider. This can limit your options when choosing cloud service providers. So when using this approach, you can become dependent on third-party services, which means vendor lock-in can be a problem. Building a system on top of a service provided by another company means that the fate of the application is now tied to the fate of the company. If the company gets acquired, goes bankrupt, or changes its business model, you might be left with an app that can't run anywhere without significant changes. Evaluating the business goals and long-term stability of a company offering these services is just as important as the technical merits.

---

1. https://en.wikipedia.org/wiki/CAP_theorem

Odd Logs

Any remaining operational concerns, like application logging, can take an unfamiliar form when using a serverless approach. When you route all your requests through one server, it's easy to log them all to see what users are doing. Without this centralization, logging must be done from the various web services that support the application. These kinds of logs are in a different format than most application server logs, and they contain data that you may not be familiar with. We'll take a closer look at analyzing web service logs in *Analyzing S3 Logs*, on page 160.

Different Security Model

With a serverless app, some common security risks disappear, but you'll encounter new issues that may be unfamiliar. For example, validating user data for security purposes cannot be performed safely in the browser. You have to assume that malicious users may commandeer the credentials in the browser to try to use any web service that the credentials allow them to access. When using a serverless approach, this means you cannot mix your application validation logic in the browser with validation done for security reasons. You have to do it separately.

Many web services provided by Amazon have facilities to validate requests. You'll see how to do this with DynamoDB in *Data Access and Validation*, on page 109. However, it may be difficult for some applications to enforce sufficient validity constraints using only the tools provided in the web service. For example, when you are writing directly from the browser, you cannot safely encode data written to a database to ensure it isn't attempting to perform a cross-site scripting attack, because the attacker can just add the data directly to the database without using the app.

In that case, you have (at least) two options. First, you can just assume that certain user-writable tables may contain unvalidated data, and design the rest of the system accordingly. For example, if the users can only write data that they alone can read, this is a viable option. Second, you can delegate those particular write operations to a custom web service, such as a Lambda function, to perform the validation and write in a secure fashion. We'll cover creating a custom web service in Chapter 6, *Building (Micro)Services with Lambda*, on page 113.

Different Identity Model

External identity management is a distinguishing feature of the app we'll build in this tutorial. Managing identity by using a web service has a lot of advantages, but the mechanisms may be unfamiliar to you. Rather than storing user profiles alongside the rest of your data, these profiles will reside in other data stores that you access separately. When building a serverless app this way, some familiar techniques for dealing with user data in databases (joining in a User table with an ID, for example) may no longer apply.

Loss of Control

Additionally, routing all requests through a middle tier provides a certain level of control that can be useful in some situations. For example, denial-of-service and other attacks can sometimes be stopped at the application server. Giving up direct control over issuing identities might also be a scary prospect for you. We'll devote an entire chapter to security concerns later, in Chapter 7, *Serverless Security*, on page 137.

Big Scale: Big Money?

Lastly, you need to understand the costs of these services. While being able to scale an app automatically is powerful, making scaling easy also means we've made spending easy. You need to understand how the prices of these services are structured and how they change as you add users. We'll examine costs of our app in depth in *Costs of the Cloud*, on page 169.

Now that you understand the trade-offs of a serverless web app, we can start the tutorial and dive into how they work. As we move through the tutorial together, you may uncover other benefits or limitations that are specific to the kinds of web applications you want to build. Once you have the complete picture, you'll be able to make an informed decision about whether this approach is applicable to your next project.

Using Your Workspace

To learn about serverless web apps, we're going to build one—a JavaScript programming puzzle app named *LearnJS*. It will present simple programming challenges to users, then let them write an answer in JavaScript and press a button to check whether the answer is correct. When we're finished, we'll have an app that looks like the screenshot on page 9.

The trick is, we're going to build this app backward. In this chapter, we're going to deploy it. Then we're going to test it. Then we're going to add some application logic. Then after that, we're going to think about design.

Unless you're familiar with the kind of iterative and incremental development style espoused by modern practitioners (I would call it *agile*, but that's not what agile means anymore), this process might seem all wrong. How can we

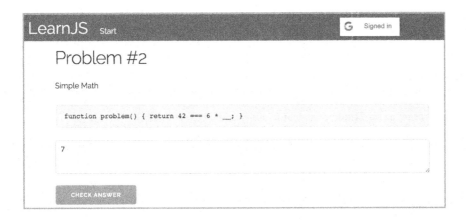

deploy our app if we haven't built it yet? How can we write automated tests before we know what we want the app to do? And shouldn't we think about the design before we start building things?

If you're skeptical, don't worry. We'll walk through the process step by step. Once we're done, you'll understand—and maybe even agree with—this approach. Not only is it a fantastic way to learn new skills, but it's also an effective way to build software: take one small step, evaluate where you are, and repeat until your customers are singing your praises.

Using Git for Source Control

Git is a source control system. Like all source control systems, Git's job is to help you track changes to your code, keep it safe, and share it with other people. If you're not familiar with it, here are the basics:

Forking a project means you make a copy for yourself. If you create an account on Github.com and then browse to our workspace project,[a] you should see a button labeled Fork in the upper-right corner. Click it, and after a few seconds, GitHub will have created a copy of this project just for you. Now you need to copy it down to your computer. This process is called *cloning*. Using a Git client, you can clone the workspace to a directory on your computer. Once that's done, you're ready to go.

To learn more about using Git and GitHub, check out GitHub Guides.[b]

---

a.   https://github.com/benrady/learnjs
b.   https://guides.github.com

To get started, you need to fork the prepared workspace, available on Github.com.[2] Using this workspace will keep you focused on building and learning, rather than setting up necessary but irrelevant infrastructure. Before moving on to the next step, clone your forked workspace using a command like this (substituting your GitHub username):

```
$ git clone git@github.com:<your username>/learnjs.git
```

To understand where we're going, we first need to understand where we are. The workspace you just cloned includes a public directory that contains an empty application. This application has no behavior, and what little markup it has will soon be replaced, but it includes all the essential tools we'll need.

As we build our application, we're primarily going to make changes to three files under the public directory: index.html, app.js, and app_spec.js. We'll add the markup for our application in index.html. This is the "single page" in our single page web app. Using your favorite text editor, open up this file and take a look. Looking at the <head> element, you can see the libraries we have to work with in the prepared workspace.

```
<head>
  <meta charset='utf-8'>
  <title>Learn JS!</title>
  <link rel='stylesheet'
    type='text/css'
    href='//fonts.googleapis.com/css?family=Raleway:400,300,600'>
  <link rel='stylesheet'
    href='https://cdnjs.cloudflare.com/ajax/libs/normalize/3.0.2/normalize.min.css'>
  <link rel='stylesheet'
    href='https://cdnjs.cloudflare.com/ajax/libs/skeleton/2.0.4/skeleton.min.css'>
  <script src='https://code.jquery.com/jquery-2.1.4.min.js'></script>
  <script src='/vendor.js'></script>
  <script src='/app.js'></script>
  <style type="text/css" media="all">
    body { margin-top: 30px; }
  </style>
</head>
```

The first library in our app is the *Normalize* CSS reset, which ensures our base style is the same across all browsers. We'll pair that with *Skeleton*, a responsive CSS boilerplate. Skeleton provides a responsive grid and a few small CSS utilities we'll use for style and layout. We've included Skeleton's default font, *Raleway*, served via Google Fonts. The next library we have is jQuery 2. We'll use jQuery for many different things, such as building application views, visual effects, and listening to events.

---

2.   https://github.com/benrady/learnjs

The next file, vendor.js, includes libraries that are either customized to our app or aren't popular enough to be available on a content delivery network (CDN). For now, the only thing in this file is a custom subset of the JavaScript library for Amazon Web Services[3] (version 2.2.4) with the following service libraries:

- CognitoIdentity
- CognitoSync
- DynamoDB
- Lambda
- STS

The next entry in the <head> element is a script called app.js. Currently, this file is empty. This is where we'll add our application logic, written in Java-Script. It will include not only the domain-specific logic of our app, but also infrastructure such as the router, template functions, and code for data binding.

The last entry in the <head> is a <style> element that currently holds our application's CSS rules. While you might want to pull these rules out into their own file at some point, having them inline for now keeps things simple.

The <body> of the application currently has a simple header and some text. We'll be replacing this shortly with a title page. By the time we're finished with this tutorial, the <body> element will hold all the markup in our application. This markup will define all our user interfaces and application views.

learnjs/1000/public/index.html
```html
<body>
  <div class='container'>
    <h1>It works!</h1>
    <div>
      <span>You're ready to start!</span>
      <span>Skeleton 2, jQuery 2, and AWS libraries are included.</span>
    </div>
  </div>
</body>
```

The workspace also includes a testing framework that is named Jasmine. The public/tests directory in our workspace contains a test runner, and an empty test suite is located at public/tests/app_spec.js. As we write tests to drive out the behavior of our application, we'll add them here.

---

3. https://sdk.amazonaws.com/builder/js/

Running Locally

Now that we understand where we are, let's start up our application and look at it, just as the user would see it. Then we can evaluate it, make a small change, and deploy our first version. To do that, you'll need to get a web server running locally that can serve the application.

The prepared workspace provides a wrapper script called sspa. We'll use this script throughout the tutorial to perform simple tasks, including configuring AWS services, building code bundles, and deploying our application. This script is written for easy reading, so feel free to open it up and take a look if you're wondering what it does. To start a local development server that serves the content of the public directory, run the following command in a terminal from the prepared workspace root directory:

```
learnjs $ ./sspa server
```

The server action in the sspa script launches a simple Python web server that serves static content. You can use your own web server, if you like. Just serve the public directory from the prepared workspace, and you're all set. Nothing that we do in this tutorial will require using any specific web app development tools. No matter what kinds of tools you prefer, you'll be able to apply the techniques in this book in the environment where you're most comfortable.

Once you've got the web server up and running, take a look at our application. If you're using the server in the prepared workspace, you can open your favorite browser and go to http://localhost:9292. You should then see something that looks like this:

It works!

You're ready to start! Skeleton 2, jQuery 2, and AWS Libraries are included.

This is our app. There's not much to it. We *could* try to plan out a long list of features for our app now, but since we don't know exactly what we want yet, planning too far ahead seems futile. Instead, we're going to add a title page to our application, and after that, we'll decide what to do next.

Creating a Landing Page

When users load our app for the first time, we want to show them a page that both quickly explains what our app is and provides a clear path to get started

LiveReload and LivePage

Whichever web server you use, I highly recommend that you use some kind of automated page-reloading tool as you work. Many different options are available. A simple one that works well with our prepared workspace is the *LivePage* plugin for Google Chrome.[a] You can install and use it easily, and it will be sufficient to run tests and reload the app whenever you make changes. A tool like this creates a fast feedback loop that you can use to inspect style and layout changes or run in-browser tests.

Another option is a tool called LiveReload. LiveReload is a both a stand-alone web server and a protocol that is used to reload web apps automatically during development. Whenever the server detects that a file on the disk has changed, it communicates the change to a JavaScript library (or browser plugin) in the client. LiveReload comes in many forms. There's the LiveReload app[b] and command-line tools like LiveReloadX[c]. If you want something you can run from Node.js, live-server[d] or grunt-livereload[e] might better suit your needs.

---

a.   https://chrome.google.com/webstore/detail/livepage/pilnojpmdoofaelbinaeodfpjheijkbh?hl=en
b.   https://github.com/livereload/LiveReload
c.   http://nitoyon.github.io/livereloadx/
d.   https://github.com/tapio/live-server
e.   https://www.npmjs.com/package/grunt-livereload

with it. A page like this is often called a *landing page*, and we're going to add one to our application.

To build our landing page, we're going to create a simple layout using the Skeleton grid. This page will contain some title text, an image, and a button often referred to as a *call to action*. Users will click this button to start using our app.

If you're not familiar with Skeleton, now's a great time to check it out.[4] There's really not much to it (hence the name). The documentation is well structured, and there are a lot of examples, so it's an easy read. Taking five minutes to go through it now will give you a good understanding of what it can do and how it works.

To lay out the grid, we're going to steal shamelessly from the Skeleton landing page example.[5] Using your text editor, open index.html and add this markup to the <body> of our application page:

---

4.   http://getskeleton.com/
5.   http://getskeleton.com/examples/landing/

learnjs/1100/public/index.html

```
<body>
  <div class='container'>
    <div class='row'>
      <div class='one-half column'>
        <h3>Learn JavaScript, one puzzle at a time.</h3>
        <a href='' class='button button-primary'>Start Now!</a>
      </div>
      <div class='one-half column'>
        <img src='/images/HeroImage.jpg' />
      </div>
    </div>
  </div>
</body>
```

In your browser, you should now see our landing page in place of the text that was there before. Clicking the button won't actually do anything, but that's OK.

Now that we've added a landing page, we have something to deploy. It's not much, but it's enough to go through the deploy process and iron out any wrinkles before we start adding more functionality to our app.

Deploying to Amazon S3

When starting a new project, you are often faced with many unknown risks. Problems that you're not even aware of can be sitting out there, waiting to suck away hours of your time. Being able to identify and avoid those risks can save you frustration, headache, and pain.

One of the risks you can avoid easily is that of deployment. We don't want to wait until we're "finished" before we deploy. Our assumptions about how things work might be wrong. As we build on top of these incorrect assumptions, the risks and potential pain grow. Web apps often suffer from these problems because we develop them on a desktop but deploy them on a server. The two environments can be totally different, and until you understand all the differences, you're potentially building on sand.

By deploying now, we'll know that our deploy process is configured correctly. We'll be able to check that the production environment is actually accessible, and that we don't have any permission problems waiting to bite us. Most importantly, we'll have gotten these necessary tasks out of the way and proven that we can take the application all the way to *done*. Until your application is in the hands of your users, from their perspective, you haven't really done anything...no matter how much code you've written.

Rather than trying to run our own web server like Apache or Nginx, we're going to deploy our app to Amazon's Simple Storage Service (S3). One of its many uses is as a static website host. While not as fully featured as other hosting options, it's inexpensive to use (typically costing just a few pennies a month) and scales well. Since we're trying to avoid the time and cost of setting up server infrastructure, S3 meets our needs perfectly.

Setting Up the AWS Command-Line Interface

As we move through this tutorial, we'll need to interact with Amazon Web Services to create and configure the services we need for our application. One great way to do this is by using the AWS command-line interface, sometimes called simply *AWS CLI*. We'll first use this tool to create our S3 bucket, and we'll get a lot more use out of it later in this book as we build our application.

If you don't have this tool installed and configured with administrator access already, you'll need to do that now. Amazon recommends that you install awscli using pip, a Python package manager. If you don't have pip installed, you can install it using easy_install, a Python package manager. You'll need Python 2.7 or later. Depending on what you already have installed, run some (or all) of the following commands:

```
$ sudo easy_install pip
$ sudo pip install awscli
```

On Debian/Ubuntu systems, you can install pip using apt instead of easy_install, like so:

```
$ sudo apt-get install python-pip
```

AWS Command-Line Interface on OS X 10.11

If you have trouble installing awscli with pip on OS X 10.11 (El Capitan), you may have to add the --upgrade and --ignore-installed six options to the install command.[a]

---

a.   https://github.com/aws/aws-cli/issues/1522#issuecomment-159007931

To use this tool, you'll need to configure it. To do that, you'll need to create a user that has administrative access to your AWS account.

Creating an AWS User with Access Keys

The Amazon Web Service that grants you access to all the other Amazon Web Services is called *Identity and Access Management*, or simply IAM. You can use this service to create individual users who have access to the services under your account. Obviously, this can be useful when working with a team, but it can also make sense to create different users by role or task. Segmenting access like this can limit the exposure of compromised keys, prevent test data from making its way into a production database, or prevent one application from accidentally interfering with another.

While you may want to create many users for your applications, the first user we're going to create is an administrative user. This user will have access to all the services in your account, so you'll have to use it carefully. To create this user, follow these steps:

1. Open the Amazon Web Services console,[6] creating an account if necessary.

2. Click the Identity & Access Management service under Security & Identity.

3. In the left sidebar, click Users.

4. Click Create New Users to create a user. We'll use this user account to deploy our app.

5. Pick a name for your user (for example, *learnjs*) and fill in the first row.

6. Ensure that the "Generate an access key for each user" check box is checked, and click Create.

7. Download the credentials when prompted.

The credentials are made up of two keys: an *access key* and a *secret key*. Both of these keys will be in the CSV file you download, or you can view them

---

6.   http://console.aws.amazon.com

directly on the Amazon website. Amazon only gives you one chance to do this, so get them now. Otherwise, you'll have to re-create the keys.

 You'll never need to provide a password for this user.

Once you get these keys, you can finish setting up AWS CLI. Run the aws configure command with the admin profile, and enter the keys when prompted. When it asks you for a default region, enter us-east-1.

```
$ aws configure --profile admin
AWS Access Key ID [None]: JFAKEKEYSRRETDMAAKIA
AWS Secret Access Key [None]: 2Jdw+ThI5iSafAKeKeY4ExamPLEsHAONXn32Af/sm
Default region name [None]: us-east-1
Default output format [None]:
```

 Joe asks:
What if I Want to Use a Different Region?

If you're familiar with AWS, you might have existing services already configured for a region other than us-east-1. While you can certainly enter other regions when configuring the admin profile, be aware that not all services work in all regions. Additionally, the sspa script may not handle URLs and other resources names correctly in other regions.

If you choose to use a region other than us-east-1, you'll need to verify that the service you're using is available in that region. You might also need to make modifications to the sspa script to accommodate your region name.

Now that you've configured AWS CLI, you should have a new file in your home directory at ~/.aws/credentials. The contents of the file should look like this (with different key values, of course):

```
[admin]
aws_access_key_id =  JFAKEKEYSRRETDMAAKIA
aws_secret_access_key =  2Jdw+ThI5iSafAKeKeY4ExamPLEsHAONXn32Af/sm
```

Now that you've created a user and saved the credentials, you'll need to grant this user permission to perform actions by creating an *access policy*. Go back to the user list in the AWS console; you should see your newly created user there. Click the user to get to the user summary page; it should look something like the screenshot on page 18.

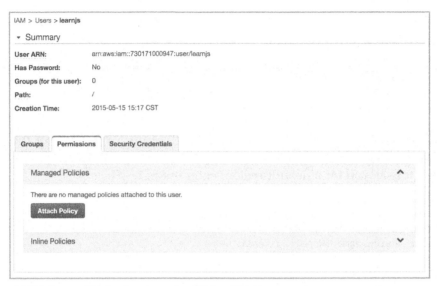

Now you need to create a policy that specifies which services this user can access. Find the Permissions section of the user summary page and click the link to attach a new managed policy. You'll then be presented with a list of policies like the following.

Check the box next to AdministratorAccess, then click the Attach Policy button, and you're all set. Now you're ready to create an S3 bucket. After that, you'll be able to deploy the application!

Creating an S3 Bucket

Now that you have an administrative user, you can create an S3 bucket. The sspa script in the prepared workspace wraps up the AWS CLI commands that not only create the bucket, but also configure it to act as a static web host capable of serving our application. If you have a hostname you'd like to use for this app, it's important that you enter that as the bucket name (for

AWS Key Safety

The user you just created has permission to perform any action on your AWS account, so it's important that you keep these keys safe. Similar to SSH private keys, these keys can be used to impersonate you. It's essential that you never share them or check them into source control.

example, learnjs.benrady.com). Otherwise, use any name you like. Just call sspa with the create_bucket action and your new bucket name as the parameter.

```
learnjs $ ./sspa create_bucket learnjs.benrady.com
make_bucket: s3://learnjs.benrady.com/
Website endpoint is: \
  http://learnjs.benrady.com.s3-website-us-east-1.amazonaws.com
```

 Amazon S3 bucket names are global, so you can't pick a name someone else is using.

If that command completes successfully, you'll know the new bucket has been created. You'll probably want to run this again with a slightly different bucket name to create a test or staging environment for your app. When the command exits, in your terminal you should see the sspa script print the URL for the bucket's website endpoint. Make note of this URL, then run the following command to deploy the app:

```
$ ./sspa deploy_bucket learnjs.benrady.com
```

And that's it! Now, take the website endpoint that the sspa script just printed out, and enter it in your browser; you should see our app. It's alive! If you don't see your app, you can double-check the website endpoint in the AWS web console for Amazon S3. If you configured AWS CLI with a region other than us-east-1, it's possible the URL printed by the sspa command was incorrect.

Once you've confirmed the app is deployed, you can clean up the URL by giving the app its own domain name. To do this, you'll need to map the domain name to the S3 bucket. You can do this by creating a CNAME entry with your DNS provider that uses the endpoint URL as the value for the record. For more detailed instructions on how to do this, refer to Appendix 2, *Assigning a Domain Name*, on page 179. Once that's complete, the deployment will be done, and we'll be ready to move on to the next step.

First Deployment

You've successfully deployed all the way to production. Now that you've done this at least once, you can have confidence that you can do it again for every forthcoming change. This will help you work in small steps, focusing on what you can do to make your app better and getting it out to the customers who might want to use it.

Next Steps

Now that you understand how to deploy an app to Amazon S3, here are some additional topics you might want to investigate.

AWS Regions

> All AWS services run in data centers located in multiple locations around the world, called *regions*. Running your application in parallel across multiple regions is a great way to ensure high availability, even in the face of catastrophic failure or natural disaster.
>
> When choosing a region, first ensure that the services you need are available in that region. You'll also want to consider things like where your users are located and where any supporting non-AWS servers are located (like email servers, for example).

Creating a Test Environment

> We just touched on it in this chapter, but as you work through this tutorial, you may want to set up a complete test environment, configured the same way as the production environment. Since it's just a tutorial, you can easily make an argument that it's not worth it, but going through the process will help you understand some of the configuration issues you run into when supporting two environments. Whether you try to figure that out now or leave it for later is a judgment call you'll need to make.

IAM Lockdown

> The administrative user we created for this app has access to every service in your account. Once you get more familiar with the services you need (and don't need), it makes sense to remove the blanket administrator policy for this user and add some more fine-grained policies, to only allow it access to the services it actually needs.

Now we're ready to move on to bigger and better things. In the next chapter, we'll add a client-side router to our application, support multiple application views, and do something about that button that doesn't work!

CHAPTER 2

Routing Views with Hash Events

In the last chapter, we deployed the first version of our web application...but it's really more of a static website. The call to action button doesn't do anything, and we only have one view. We need to add more views to our app, but we also need these views to be dynamic, responding to the user's actions and providing an interactive experience.

On a static website, the content on each page is fixed, and navigation is controlled through hyperlinks to other pages. Traditional MVC web frameworks improve this by using a server-side router that associates URLs with *controllers*, which use *views* and *models* to create dynamic content. Single page apps improve upon this even further by moving the routing logic into the browser and eliminating the round-trip request to the server. This makes a client-side router an essential component of any single page web app. By creating a router, we can support multiple views in the application, while only loading a single HTML page.

You may be wondering how our router is going to avoid making a request to a web server. After all, the web is built out of hyperlinked documents...how can we move from one view to the next without fetching a new page? It has been a long-standing policy of web browsers that when a user clicks a link that contains just a hash tag (like #home), that tag is added to the URL but the page doesn't reload. This hash tag is often referred to as the URL's *hash*.

Using JavaScript, we can listen for the event that is triggered by the browser when the hash changes. We can take advantage of this browser behavior to build a router for our single page app. When the URL's hash changes, the router looks up a function that creates the markup we want to display to the user. This lets us keep the application loaded while the user's view changes, and it lets us still maintain the familiar metaphor of a URL that the user can save, bookmark, copy, or share.

In this chapter, we'll build a router that will use these *hash events* to trigger the creation and display of dynamic markup. The router will use predefined *routes* that associate URL hashes with *view functions*. These view functions will create the markup and behavior for the views. This will not only let us add routes to the application to create new views, but it will give us an easy way to navigate across them. Once we have the router working, we'll get the application loaded by listening to an event using jQuery. By the end of this chapter, we will have successfully turned our website into a true single page web *application.*

Designing a Testable Router

Although there are some exceptions, it's generally not possible to run AWS services on your local workstation. With all of our application's back end running in AWS, you might be worried that it will be difficult to test. If we want to create a fast feedback loop that tells us if things are working, we're going to need to diverge from the traditional approach of running a complete service stack in a development environment in order to test the application while we build it. Instead, we're going to test our router using unit tests written with a *test first* approach. Designing the router by writing the tests first will ensure the resulting design is easy to test. Although our focus on testing will be limited to this chapter, you'll be able to apply these same techniques throughout the rest of the book.

The design of the router has a profound impact on the overall testability of the application, which is why we're starting there. We want to create a suite of automated tests that can quickly check if our app is working, without being dependent on back-end services to run the tests. To build the router, we're going to drive out its behavior incrementally with tests. We'll write these tests one at a time, in parallel with the application, to ensure that all of the code is testable. We'll eschew testing entire workflows and focus instead on testing small bits of behavior to create tests that run in a few milliseconds. We'll be able to avoid race conditions and other timing problems in the tests because they won't need to make asynchronous requests to a server.

One way to create a testable application is to build "seams" into the design—in other words, clear boundaries where tests can easily invoke behavior, inspect output, and simulate interaction. One seam in our application is the markup. If we make the markup available to the tests, they can inspect it. Encapsulating the JavaScript creates another seam. Making the JavaScript accessible to the tests means they can invoke it to verify behavior. The browser itself can act as a seam, allowing our tests to simulate user actions by triggering events. You can see some of these testing seams in this diagram.

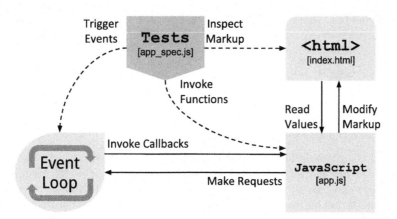

Creating an application that is easily tested naturally promotes decoupling,[1] which improves the design. As we build the router, we'll also use these tests to improve the design of the code through *refactoring*. We'll work incrementally to ensure that we only add what we absolutely need, which will keep the code as simple as it can be. The result should be a reliable suite of tests that support a simple, functional, and easily testable application.

Running Jasmine Tests

To write the tests, we're going to use the *Jasmine* testing framework. Jasmine is similar to RSpec and most xUnit frameworks, so if you've used any of those before, you should be comfortable. If not, you can follow along, or you can check out the Jasmine documentation first.[2] It's pretty simple once you get the pattern.

The prepared workspace includes a test runner. If you have the application loaded, add /tests/index.html to the URL, and you should see the test output. For now, it should say we have no tests. Also, just like the rest of the application, using the LivePage plugin or a LiveReload server means this page will reload automatically as you make changes to the app or tests.

---

1. https://en.wikipedia.org/wiki/Coupling_(computer_programming)
2. http://jasmine.github.io

Running Tests in Production

When someone reports a bug, and you can't reproduce it anywhere, how do you fix it? People often interpret "Works on my machine" as an accusation that the bug being reported isn't real—that somehow, the user is creating the problem instead of the software. When I say that to someone, it's actually a call for help. Not being able to reproduce a problem leaves me stymied. After all, if I can't reproduce it, how will I know when it's fixed?

When you find yourself in this situation, you can use the test suite as a sanity check to ensure your assumptions about the app still hold true, even in environments you can't access directly. The deploy script in the prepared workspace not only deploys the application to production, but deploys the tests as well. This means you can run the tests from any device where you can run the app.

So if you have a user who's reporting a problem, a quick way to troubleshoot what's going on can be to ask the user to browse to /tests and make sure they all pass. If they don't, the user can copy and paste the output and send it to you. You can then try to reproduce the failing test as a proxy for reproducing the error that the user is reporting.

Jasmine organizes tests by enclosing them in callbacks passed to two functions: describe and it. The it function is used to write individual tests, while the describe function allows us to add context and setup around the tests. We're going to add one outer describe to hold all the tests for the app, and then add an it for the test we want to write.

Writing the First Test

Before we can write a test, we need to figure out what behavior we want. Expressing this behavior in plain English—and naming the test accordingly—will make it clear what's going on when we come back to it later. Test names should focus on why the code does what it does, rather than how it does it.

The reason we need a router is to support multiple views in the application. Right now, the landing page is our only view. To drive out the router behavior, we'll write a test that asserts that there's another view that can be created. This will not only help us create the functionality we want, but it will clearly explain why it's needed.

The second view we're going to create will show the programming problems in the app, so we're going to call it the *problem view*. This will be the primary view that users interact with in the app. We're not really sure what we want it to look like yet, but we can at least add enough behavior to the app to get it to transition from the landing page to this new view. Being able to do this is a small step that will help us make progress...even if the new view doesn't have any real content.

Jasmine will combine the text in the describe and it functions to create the full name of the test. We want to ensure those names are readable. The name of Jasmine's it function also gives us a hint about how to name the test. You should be able to read it, like "It can show a problem view." In the prepared workspace, open public/tests/app_spec.js and add the new test there.

learnjs/2000/public/tests/app_spec.js

```
describe('LearnJS', function() {
  it('can show a problem view', function() {
  });
});
```

Now that we have a name for our test, we can write the test itself. The action we're going to take in this test is to invoke a JavaScript function that we'll call the *router function*. The router function's job is to find and display the appropriate view, given the current route as defined by the URL's hash. We're going to call this function showView and put it in a *namespace*[3] called learnjs. This function will be responsible for creating the view markup and adding that markup to our app. It will take the URL hash as a parameter, which it will use to select the view. For this test, we'll pass in a hash value that represents the route for the first problem in our app: #problem-1.

The showView function doesn't exist yet, but that's OK. We're using the test to drive out the design of the function. The figure on page 26 shows our first pass at building a router. Note that there's nothing in our app that will call our router function. Eventually, another part of our app will invoke showView() when the browser fires a hashchange event. It will pass in the current hash value provided by the document location API,[4] using window.location.hash. When showView is invoked, we'll create the view and append it to the page.

The assertion we're going to make in our test is that the router has placed the problem view markup in a *view container*. The view container is another essential part of our router. It's the element the router will use to hold the view's markup. Any markup inside the view container will be replaced when the router adds a new view.

---

3. http://eloquentjavascript.net/10_modules.html#h_NitCO6r9Hn
4. https://developer.mozilla.org/en-US/docs/Web/API/Window/location

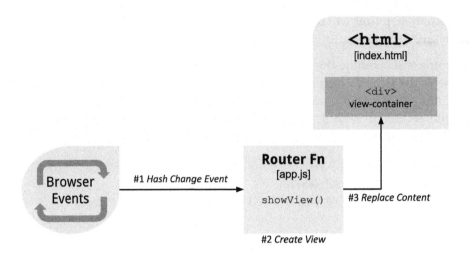

To write the assertion, we're going to use jQuery to select[5] elements from our page. We'll assert that our app contains an element with the view-container class, and inside that element is another element with the problem-view class. We do this by selecting these elements with jQuery, then asserting that the number of elements we selected is equal to one.

learnjs/2100/public/tests/app_spec.js

```
describe('LearnJS', function() {
  it('can show a problem view', function() {
    learnjs.showView('#problem-1');
    expect($('.view-container .problem-view').length).toEqual(1);
  });
});
```

If your LivePage/LiveReload is working properly, when you save the spec file the test runner should reload and run the tests, showing you the test fails:

```
1 spec, 1 failure
LearnJS can show a problem view
ReferenceError: learnjs is not defined
```

This test fails as we expect. We haven't added any behavior to our app, nor have we created the namespace where our application is going to live. The first step in getting this test to pass will be to do that.

---

5.   https://learn.jquery.com/using-jquery-core/selecting-elements/

The Router Function

Now that we've got a failing test, we can write the router function. To get our router test to pass, we have to add three things. We need to create a view container in the markup to give the router a place to add the views. We need to create the showView function and have it create a minimal version of the problem view. Lastly, we need to create a namespace where our router function—and the rest of our application—can live. Once those things are complete, we'll have the first version of our router in place. All it will be able to do is switch from one view to another, but that's a good start.

Since our test is complaining about not being able to find the learnjs namespace, we're going to start with that.

Creating a Namespace

You might be wondering why we need a namespace at all. While we could define showView by itself, when building our application we must avoid accidentally using function and variable names that are already defined in the global scope. We call these *name collisions*, and they can be a real problem. By containing our application in a namespace, we can prevent name collisions and ensure our app works with current and future browsers.

The JavaScript runtime environment provided by all major browsers includes a number of different APIs. To access these APIs, browsers define a window object as a sort of top-level entry point. You can reference this object to make API calls. For example, you can get the current URL by calling window.location.toString(), and you can programmatically navigate in the browser by assigning window.location to a URL string.

In addition to being the access point for the browser APIs, the window object is the container for all global variables. This is convenient in that you don't have to prefix all of your API calls with window, because they are essentially global. For example, in place of using window.location.toString(), you can use location.toString(). Unfortunately, this also means that any global names you create might collide with names in the APIs. Even if you're sure that your current names won't collide, it's hard to predict what new APIs browser makers will introduce.

Fortunately, there's a simple way to avoid this problem. We can create a *namespace* for our application. A namespace is just a JavaScript object that we can use to hold the parts of our application. This namespace is the first thing we'll add to our app.js file.

learnjs/2100/public/app.js

```
'use strict';
var learnjs = {};
```

See? Nothing to it. This simple but powerful technique provides some structure to our application and helps avoid name collisions. We can add our application's functions and variables to this object without having to worry if our application names will collide with names on the global window object, or any global names defined by any of our libraries.

We've also included the 'use strict'; statement here to tell the browser to enforce stricter rules when evaluating our JavaScript. This means that rather than ignoring problems, we'll get a nice error telling us what went wrong. Since we've put this statement at the top of app.js, we're only enforcing strict mode for our code and any code loaded after it.

Adding the Router Function

Our test is still failing, but now that we've created a namespace for our application, the error message is different.

```
1 spec, 1 failure
LearnJS can show a problem view
  TypeError: learnjs.showView is not a function
```

Here, the test is complaining that learnjs.showView isn't a function. That's true…it's undefined,[6] because we haven't created it yet. We have two more steps to make our test pass, and this is one of them. Since our test is complaining about not being able to find the showView function, we'll do that next.

This means the first function we'll add to our application namespace will be the showView() function. In this function, we'll use jQuery to select the view-container element and append the view markup to it. We haven't created a separate function for the problem view yet, so to start, we'll just hard-code this function to append a <div> with the problem-view class, because that's all this test requires. We'll add the showView() implementation to our namespace in app.js.

learnjs/2100/public/app.js

```
'use strict';
var learnjs = {};
learnjs.showView = function(hash) {
  var problemView = $('<div class="problem-view">').text('Coming soon!');
  $('.view-container').empty().append(problemView);
}
```

---

6. http://eloquentjavascript.net/01_values.html#h_WAVjYN+DYj

Joe asks:

Am I Really Going to Create the View Markup Like This?

Although it's possible—and sometimes useful—to create markup dynamically with jQuery, creating large amounts of markup with nothing but jQuery can be a bit tedious. The first implementation of showView() does this, but this implementation isn't going to last long.

When this is added, the failure message of our test changes:

```
1 spec, 1 failure
LearnJS can show a problem view
Expected 0 to equal 1.
```

You want to avoid adding anything else to the problem view at this point. You'll add functionality to it later (with tests). For now, you need to focus on driving out the behavior of the router. The good news is, you're getting closer, because the assertion in our test is now failing as you expect.

Creating a View Container

Before, this test was raising JavaScript errors. Now it's actually failing the assertion. All the code is executing without error; it's just that the test sees zero elements when it expected one. These are the kinds of failures we want out of our tests. They're specific, and they lead us to what we need to do next.

In this case, although our showView function is creating and appending markup, there's no view container in the page for it to append it to, so when we call jQuery's append function, the markup goes nowhere. To fix this, we're going to have to make two changes to our markup. We'll have to create the view container. We'll also need to introduce a new element into our application that will give our tests access to the markup in our application.

Right now, our tests have no way to access the markup in our app. The test runner at tests/index.html is a different document than our app in index.html. There's a way to bring them together, but we're going to need to add something to our app to do it.

In our prepared workspace, our test runner has a file named public/tests/SpecHelper.js. This file has some code that copies any markup in our application that's contained in an element with the markup class. It then takes that markup and appends it to the body of the test runner's page, making it available to all of our tests. To make our view container—and all of our application's markup—visible from our tests, you need to create this element.

While you're doing this, you also need to add the view-container class to the <div> with the Skeleton container class on it. We're going to make this our view container element. Since we're making our view container a Skeleton container, our views can create their markup with rows and columns from the Skeleton grid, knowing that the content will be placed properly in a container.

Once you make both of these changes, the <body> of our application's index.html file will look like this:

learnjs/2100/public/index.html

```
<body>
  <div class='markup'>
    <div class='view-container container'>
      <div class='row'>
        <div class='one-half column'>
          <h3>Learn JavaScript, one puzzle at a time.</h3>
          <a href='' class='button button-primary'>Start Now!</a>
        </div>
        <div class='one-half column'>
          <img src='/images/HeroImage.jpg'/>
        </div>
      </div>
    </div>
  </div>
</body>
```

Once you save that change, our test should run.

```
1 spec, 0 failure
LearnJS can show a problem view
```

Now our test is passing! We've taken some important steps here. We've written our first automated test and made it pass. We've created a router function that lets our application navigate between multiple views without reloading. We've created a view container that all of our views can use to enclose their markup. Lastly, we've made all of our application markup visible to our tests, making it easy for us to test our views and their UI elements.

If you don't feel comfortable writing Jasmine tests yet, don't worry. We've only started to use them in our app, so you don't need to be an expert. Rather than having me spend a lot of time telling you everything Jasmine can do for you, let's move forward, and you'll *see* what it can do along the way. The tests are important to us, and while we expect to get back much more value than the effort we put in to writing them, we want to stay focused on building our app. After all, you don't make customers happy by writing tests; you make them happy by delivering software that excites and delights them.

Adding Routes

Our router is now capable of showing a second view, but that's really all it does. The showView() function is hardcoded to just show the problem view. To fix this, we need to create something that lets our router associate hashes with view functions. Each of these associations is called a *route*, and we're going to add one to our application now.

Our routes are going to be represented by a JavaScript object that acts as a lookup for the hash values we expect. This object will hold the associations between URL hash names and view functions. The view functions will return jQuery objects that contain the markup for our view. Right now, we only need one route, but we can add more views to our app by adding more entries to the routes object.

Adding the routes object will allow us to pull the view creation behavior out into individual functions, as shown in this figure. The router now works in four steps. Hash change events still trigger the router function showView, but the router now invokes decoupled view functions to create the views, which are then appended to the page. Being able to extract the view creation logic into a function means we can test it without having to do so through the router, which would complicate our tests.

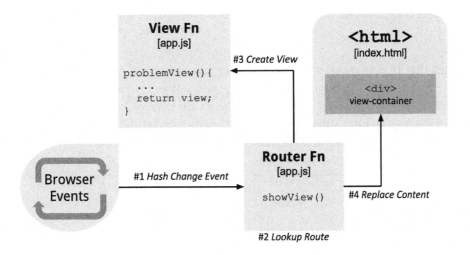

To introduce these routes, we want to create another test to drive out the behavior. While we could test the routes object directly, that would make it harder to refactor that code later. For example, if we changed the structure of the routes object but didn't change the behavior of the router, we wouldn't want our tests to fail.

Instead, we're going to write a test that uses the existing router function, showView, to assert what happens where there is no hash at all. This kind of test is sometimes referred to as the *null case* or the *default case*. This doesn't necessarily mean that we're going to use the null JavaScript keyword. Rather, it refers to a general category of interaction based on a lack of data. Empty strings, empty objects, empty arrays, and the number zero often appear in null case tests.

What we want to assert here is that when the hash is the empty string, our application shows the landing page view. The assertion in this test will be similar to our first test: attempting to select an element with jQuery and asserting that exactly one element was selected.

learnjs/2200/public/tests/app_spec.js

```
describe('LearnJS', function() {
  it('can show a problem view', function() {
    learnjs.showView('#problem-1');
    expect($('.view-container .problem-view').length).toEqual(1);
  });

  it('shows the landing page view when there is no hash', function() {
    learnjs.showView('');
    expect($('.view-container .landing-view').length).toEqual(1);
  });
});
```

To get this test to pass, we can introduce a routes object and a *view function* named problemView. The router will use the routes object to find a view function, with a fallback to the landing page if the route cannot be found. Since our landing page is just sitting in the view container by default, for now, this means we can do nothing if the hash is not matched to a route.

learnjs/2200/public/app.js

```
'use strict';

var learnjs = {};

learnjs.problemView = function() {
  return $('<div class="problem-view">').text('Coming soon!');
}

learnjs.showView = function(hash) {
```

```
  var routes = {
    '#problem-1': learnjs.problemView
  };
  var viewFn = routes[hash];
  if (viewFn) {
    $('.view-container').empty().append(viewFn());
  }
}
```

Lastly, you'll need to wrap the landing page view in a <div> with the landing-view class, so we can select it in our app and our tests.

learnjs/2200/public/index.html

```
<body>
  <div class='markup'>
    <div class='view-container container'>
      <div class='landing-view'>
        <div class='row'>
          <div class='one-half column'>
            <h3>Learn JavaScript, one puzzle at a time.</h3>
            <a href='' class='button button-primary'>Start Now!</a>
          </div>
          <div class='one-half column'>
            <img src='/images/HeroImage.jpg'/>
          </div>
        </div>
      </div>
    </div>
  </div>
</body>
```

And with that, we should have two passing tests. Clicking the call to action button on the landing page won't change the view yet, but soon we'll be able to add a href attribute with a hash to control navigation. Once the app starts listening for hash events, if the router can find a route that matches the name of this hash, it will invoke the appropriate view function to create the view, and it will replace the view-container element with the view's markup. If it can't find a matching route, it will do nothing, leaving the landing page in place.

Adding View Parameters

We've added the first route to our app, but there's something not quite right about it. This route is specific to a single problem—problem #1. We don't really want to make a new route for each problem we add to our app. We'd like to have one route (and one view) that can show any of the problems we have in our app.

To make this work, we're going to *parameterize* our views. We'll split the hash into two parts: a name and a parameter, using the dash in between as a delimiter. We'll pass the parameter to the view function when we invoke it, and the function can use that data to construct the view. We're going to call these values *view parameters*, and they will be our application's first way to add data to the views.

In this particular case, the view parameter is the problem ID, but as we build out our application, we'll be able to use view parameters for just about anything. We could pass other kinds of identifiers, such as primary database keys, UUIDs, or cryptographic hashes. We could also pass raw data, either as plain text or using a format such as encoded JSON or Rison.[7] The router will make no assumptions about what the view parameter is, how to interpret it, or how to parse it. It's the view's responsibility to know what kind of view parameters it accepts and what to do with them.

To test this behavior, we're going to introduce a new kind of test construct, called a *spy*. Spies are used to test the interactions between two pieces of code. In this case, we're going to need to test the interaction between the router and our newly created view function for the problem view.

Testing Interactions with Spies

A spy is a particular kind of *test double*. Test doubles stand in for real objects or functions and help support our tests. Some test doubles can actually make assertions about how they're used (or not used); other ones simply pretend to be something they're not. Jasmine has built-in support for spies that can stand in for functions and let us verify how the code we're trying to test interacts with other code that's outside the scope of the test.

Listen to Your Tests

You'll often hear from experienced programmers that code should be organized to "do one thing well," but what exactly is "one thing"? It's hard to measure that objectively, but tests can provide a way. Just as with our router, writing tests will often guide your design. If the setup for a test is becoming too long to read, maybe the behavior you're trying to test needs to stand on its own.

We're going to use a spy to verify the interaction between our router and the problem view function. We want to assert that the router correctly extracts the view parameter and passes it to the view function when we call our router

---

7.   https://github.com/Nanonid/rison

function. To do this, we'll use Jasmine's spyOn function, which temporarily replaces a named function with a spy. The spy records all the calls that are made to it, and we can use special Jasmine matchers like toHaveBeenCalledWith to assert that the spy was invoked with certain arguments. Once the test finishes, Jasmine replaces the spy with the original function, so none of our other tests are affected. Using a Jasmine spy, we can write a test like this:

learnjs/2300/public/tests/app_spec.js

```
it('passes the hash view parameter to the view function', function() {
  spyOn(learnjs, 'problemView');
  learnjs.showView('#problem-42');
  expect(learnjs.problemView).toHaveBeenCalledWith('42');
});
```

In this test, we needed to configure our spy by passing two parameters to spyOn. The first is the object where the function resides. In this case, it's our namespace, but you can also pass in window to spy on global functions. The second parameter is the name of the function, passed as a string. Note that when you go to make the assertion, Jasmine requires that you refer to the function directly, since it's been replaced by a spy.

After ensuring this test fails with the error "Expected spy problemView to have been called with ['42'] but it was never called," we're ready to improve showView to support view parameters. We'll split the hash into an array, then use the parts of the array to find the correct route and build our view.

learnjs/2300/public/app.js

```
    learnjs.showView = function(hash) {
      var routes = {
➤       '#problem': learnjs.problemView
      };
➤     var hashParts = hash.split('-');
➤     var viewFn = routes[hashParts[0]];
      if (viewFn) {
➤       $('.view-container').empty().append(viewFn(hashParts[1]));
      }
    }
```

That should be enough for our test to pass. Right now, the problem view doesn't do anything with the parameter that it's passed. It doesn't have any content, and we're not ready to add any yet. Next, we'll want to use this view parameter inside the problemView function.

By using a spy, we've managed to test the router's interaction with a view, without changing the view. Focusing the tests on interactions rather than workflows lets us add behavior incrementally like this. We can be confident that the view parameter is being passed correctly, even though the problem view ignores it for now.

Handling Parameters in View Functions

To complete the other half of this two-part test, we're going to add a test for the problemView function. Up until now, the code in this function has only been tested through the router function. While that's fine for one test, continuing to test the problem view like this would make the test suite *uninformative*.

Building a FIRE-y Test Suite

As I build up the suite of tests for an application, I want to hold certain properties constant. I want the suite of tests to be *Fast, Informative, Reliable*, and *Exhaustive*— or FIRE-y, for short. For example, keeping the tests *fast* means I can run them on every change, and ensuring that they are *reliable* means they won't break randomly.

In this chapter, I took what might have seemed to be a single test and broke it in half. I did that to keep the tests *informative*. When something goes wrong, I want the tests to clearly explain what it is. Having each test only verify a specific behavior of the application helps to ensure that a single bug introduced into the app will cause *exactly one* test to fail. If I've done a good job naming and organizing the tests, then the reason for the failure will be apparent immediately.

Alternatively, if I write tests for every end-to-end workflow in the app, for a particular change there may be dozens of tests that depend on that behavior. Then, if I introduce a bug or try to change something, rather than having a single test to inform me that something is wrong, I'll have a huge mess of failing tests saying *everything* is wrong. Resolving the change then becomes a tedious task of wading through all the failing tests, trying to discern what exactly is going on and what to do about it.

To verify that everything is tested when using this approach, I need to ensure my test suites are *exhaustive*. Since I don't test every workflow end-to-end, I need to test every part of every workflow independently, and then test all the interactions between those parts. This gives me confidence to build effective test suites that run in the blink of an eye.

To organize our problem view tests within the larger scope of the application, we should create a describe section for this view and put it inside the outer describe for LearnJS. Jasmine lets you nest describe functions in this manner to provide context and scope for a set of tests. When we create our test, it should look like this:

learnjs/2400/public/tests/app_spec.js

```
describe('LearnJS', function() {
  it('can show a problem view', function() {
    learnjs.showView('#problem-1');
    expect($('.view-container .problem-view').length).toEqual(1);
  });

  it('shows the landing page view when there is no hash', function() {
    learnjs.showView('');
    expect($('.view-container .landing-view').length).toEqual(1);
  });

  it('passes the hash view parameter to the view function', function() {
    spyOn(learnjs, 'problemView');
    learnjs.showView('#problem-42');
    expect(learnjs.problemView).toHaveBeenCalledWith('42');
  });

  describe('problem view', function() {
    it('has a title that includes the problem number', function() {
      var view = learnjs.problemView('1');
      expect(view.text()).toEqual('Problem #1 Coming soon!');
    });
  });
});
```

When you see a failing test, you can add this implementation to get it to pass:

learnjs/2400/public/app.js

```
learnjs.problemView = function(problemNumber) {
  var title = 'Problem #' + problemNumber + ' Coming soon!';
  return $('<div class="problem-view">').text(title);
}
```

In the next chapter, we'll improve this view, taking advantage of the view parameter that's being passed in. For now, we have a more important step to take. We need to get our application loading, so we can try it out and deploy a new and (slightly) improved version.

Loading the Application

Just like any web page, our single page app has to be loaded. Modern browsers are sophisticated when it comes to loading content from the Internet, but a simplified version of what happens goes something like this: when you enter a URL, the browser fetches the file specified in the URL and downloads it. Once the file is downloaded, if it is HTML, the browser will start downloading other assets specified in the markup, such as CSS, JavaScript, fonts, images, or videos.

> ### Joe asks:
> ## What About the Test?
>
> You may have noticed that I didn't cover how to write a test for the code in the <script> tag in our index.html. Could I? Yes...but not using techniques or tools we've discussed so far. While I could jump ahead and explain how to do this, you will inevitably find behavior in your apps that you don't know how to test effectively. Either the tests will be too complex to be useful, or you simply won't know how to test it at all. This is especially true if you're still learning how to drive out the design of your code with tests. Understanding how to deal with this is essential to using tests effectively.
>
> It would be patronizing to say that every line of code you write should be covered by an automated test. Life is rarely simple enough for dogmatic pronouncements like that to stand up over time. Rather than dogma, you're usually better served with good judgment and some reasonable guidelines. Here are a few:
>
> - Don't assume a particular implementation. It can make things hard to test. Be flexible.
>
> - Favor testability over encapsulation. The latter is nice; the former is essential.
>
> - Assume someone else knows how to test it. How could you discover their approach?
>
> - Try to write tests for untested code before you change it. Maybe you'll find a way.
>
> - When all else fails, isolate untested code from testable code.

So while our app loads like a web page, it only needs to be loaded once—like a native application. However, the loading process for a single page app is rarely complete when the browser has rendered the page. There are event listeners to be added, data structures to be initialized, and other assets to be fetched. We need a way to hook into the browser's loading process and do the additional things our app requires.

We could do this simply by sticking some JavaScript in a <script> element at the top of the page. The problem with that is that the browser might run our JavaScript as soon as it can—even before the browser has created the HTML element hierarchy. This might make it impossible to change or add elements that we'll need to create our view, because they're not in the page yet.

One way to avoid this is to attach a listener that will be notified when the page is ready. We could also add our <script> tag to the bottom of the <body> element, and most browsers will evaluate that after loading the page. In this case, we're going to go the belt-and-suspenders route and do both. We'll add a <script> tag at the end of the page that attaches a listener. To do this, we're going to use jQuery's $.ready() function.

Responding to Events

The $.ready() function is like many other jQuery event functions in that it allows you to add a listener for an event. You just need to supply a callback function as an argument, and when the event is triggered, your callback will be invoked. In this case, the event is the DOMContentLoaded event, which is triggered by the browser as soon as all the HTML has been loaded.

We'll name our callback appOnReady(), and it will be responsible for loading our application. To attach this function to the load event, we'll call $.ready() and pass in learnjs.appOnReady. We're going to do this in a <script> tag that we'll put at the bottom of the page <body> element, like this:

learnjs/2500/public/index.html

```
<body>
  <div class='markup'>
    <div class='view-container container'>
      <div class='landing-view'>
        <div class='row'>
          <div class='one-half column'>
            <h3>Learn JavaScript, one puzzle at a time.</h3>
            <a href='' class='button button-primary'>Start Now!</a>
          </div>
          <div class='one-half column'>
            <img src='/images/HeroImage.jpg'/>
          </div>
        </div>
      </div>
    </div>
  </div>
➤ <script type='text/javascript'>
➤   $(window).ready(learnjs.appOnReady);
➤ </script>
</body>
```

It's important that our markup <div> *not* include the <script> tag at the end of the <body>. Otherwise, that <script> tag will be evaluated when the tests are run, and our application will try to load. We want to have control over when (and if) our application is loaded from within the tests. Otherwise, any state that is changed during the loading process, such as the current view, might affect the result of our tests.

When the page loads, jQuery will call learnjs.appOnReady() once the page is ready, allowing our application to do what it needs to start up. Note the lack of parentheses on appOnReady when we pass it to $.ready(). We're not invoking it, just referencing it.[8] If you accidentally add those parentheses, you may get strange behavior out of your app, because it won't load at the right time.

Next, we need to add the learnjs.appOnReady() function to our app. We want this function to call our router function when the page is loaded, so we're going to use a spy to assert that showView is invoked with the current page's hash.

learnjs/2500/public/tests/app_spec.js

```
it('invokes the router when loaded', function() {
  spyOn(learnjs, 'showView');
  learnjs.appOnReady();
  expect(learnjs.showView).toHaveBeenCalledWith(window.location.hash);
});
```

Now we can add our function to the application namespace. Put it at the bottom of our app.js file.

learnjs/2500/public/app.js

```
learnjs.appOnReady = function() {
  learnjs.showView(window.location.hash);
}
```

That should make our tests pass. Now, we need to subscribe to the hashchange event, and our router will be ready for a test run.

Responding to Hash Events

We have our routes defined, and we have a way to create views. Now we can add a listener for the hashchange event. Of course, this change starts with a new test.

Rather than actually changing the hash in this test, we're going to use jQuery's trigger function to trigger the hashchange event. We're doing this because our tests run in a browser, just like our application, and changing the hash of the test runner might create problems. At a minimum, it would make the state of our tests inconsistent, because the value of the hash might be different depending on the order the tests are run in. This could make our tests *unreliable*, which is something we really want to avoid.

To trigger the event, we're going to load our app and then spy on the showView function. Spying on the function after loading the app ensures that our spy records the call to showView caused by the hashchange event, and not just when the app was loaded. After that, we're going to call trigger and pass in the name

---

8. http://eloquentjavascript.net/03_functions.html#h_y6WGSsYfER

of the event we want to trigger—in this case, hashchange. Then we can assert that our spy was invoked with the right arguments.

learnjs/2600/public/tests/app_spec.js

```
it('subscribes to the hash change event', function() {
  learnjs.appOnReady();
  spyOn(learnjs, 'showView');
  $(window).trigger('hashchange');
  expect(learnjs.showView).toHaveBeenCalledWith(window.location.hash);
});
```

Now that we have a failing test, we can add some behavior to appOnReady to make it pass. To register our listener, we're going to assign a function to the onhashchange property on the window object. The browser API provides this property, which lets us register an event handler for the hashchange event. This function will be invoked whenever the hash changes. We'll just add this listener to our appOnReady() function.

learnjs/2600/public/app.js

```
learnjs.appOnReady = function() {
  window.onhashchange = function() {
    learnjs.showView(window.location.hash);
  };
  learnjs.showView(window.location.hash);
}
```

In this function, you can see we've attached a listener. In this listener, we then call the function showView(), passing in window.location.hash, just as we do when the app is loaded. Once we make this change, our new router should work. To see it work in the application, we'll need to add an attribute to the <a> element we use for our call to action button on the landing page. We can use a hash to add a link to our problem view, so that when users click this button, they'll be taken to the first problem.

learnjs/2600/public/index.html

```
<a href='#problem-1' class='button button-primary'>Start Now!</a>
```

Now that we've added the hash change listener and a link, we can try out the app to see if we got it right. Go to the landing page and click the call to action button. That should display the stubbed-out problem view. If it does, we know that we have a functioning router and an app that can change views without making a request to an application server.

For now, we're going to deploy what we have. What's in production now is a landing page with a call to action button that doesn't work. This version is a little better. Certain things still don't work yet. For example, hitting the back button to return to the landing page doesn't do anything, but we can resolve these issues soon. Although we're not really in a position to start sharing our application with potential users, any time we've improved our app, we want to deploy it as soon as we can. While we have confidence that our app works as expected, seeing it actually work in the production environment is the only way to have *certainty*.

Deploy Again

We've added a router, and our app can respond to the call to action button. We've got a way to add new routes and a nice suite of tests to show how it all works. Go ahead and deploy the app using the same ./sspa deploy_bucket command we used in Chapter 1. After that's complete, bring up the app in a browser and give it a quick tour while we consider what's next.

Next Steps

Now that you understand how a router works, here are some additional topics you might want to investigate. To keep things simple, we won't explore them in the book, but you might want to check them out on your own before moving on to the next chapter.

Jasmine Matchers

> Jasmine has support for all kinds of *matchers*, which are the functions you call after an expect to make an assertion. Unlike the structural describe and it functions, there are lots of different kinds of matchers, and it can take a bit of time to understand how to use them all. To learn more about Jasmine matchers, visit http://jasmine.github.io. We're using version 2.0.2 here.

Jasmine-jQuery

> Jasmine is a great testing framework, but it's not strictly focused on web development. In addition to the built-in matchers provided by Jasmine, the Jasmine-jQuery extension adds a number of HTML-specific matchers, like toExist and toHaveClass, that make testing web applications easier. You can learn more about Jasmine-jQuery at https://github.com/velesin/jasmine-jquery.

Test Doubles

> We touched on how to use Jasmine spies in this chapter, but there are many different kinds of test doubles, with all sorts of uses. You can see some examples here: http://xunitpatterns.com/Test%20Double.html.

Routing Libraries

Our routing needs are pretty simple, but if yours are more complex, you might want to consider using a routing library. Director (https://github.com/flatiron/director) and Page.js (http://visionmedia.github.io/page.js/) are examples of routing libraries. If you find yourself changing our simple router too much, perhaps one of these might be a good replacement.

JavaScript Testing Alternatives

We chose Jasmine as our testing framework in this book, but there are at least a dozen other options out there, all with their own benefits and trade-offs. QUnit (http://qunitjs.com/) is a popular alternative. Sinon.js (http://sinonjs.org/) is another. Vows.js (http://vowsjs.org/) is an asynchronous testing framework that offers a different take on the problem. The techniques we discuss in this book could be used with any of these frameworks. Investigate them for yourself to decide what's right for you.

Hash Change Events

There's more to the hashchange event than what we've covered in this book. You can get the old hash value in the event callback.[9] You can also manipulate browser history using the pushState and popState methods on window.history. These can come in handy when trying to simulate more traditional methods of routing.

In the next chapter, we're going to implement our problem view. We'll look at how to use HTML templates to replace that ugly jQuery-generated markup we have. Our app will get a lot more functionality, and we'll finally deploy a version of our app that's worth sharing with users.

---

9. https://developer.mozilla.org/en-US/docs/Web/API/WindowEventHandlers/onhashchange

CHAPTER 3

Essentials of Single Page Apps

Despite what the critics may say, let there be no doubt that the modern web browser is an application container. Whether it's a good one or not is irrelevant. Web standards such as HTTP, HTML, and JavaScript are the basis for an application delivery platform available on *billions* of desktop, mobile, and tablet devices around the world. There are probably at least two of these devices within your reach right now. Building a web application is the fastest way to get your app into the hands of the most people. To take advantage of this global phenomena, we need to understand how to make the browser be the best application container it can be.

Now that we have a testable router providing the foundation, we can build out the rest of our application. In this chapter, we'll add all the remaining essential components to our app. You'll find many of these same components in any single page app you build, serverless or otherwise. Together, we'll build out the application's views, create a simple data model, and bind the data in that model to the markup. We'll see how to use visual effects to provide feedback about user input, and we'll create an application shell with a navigation bar. By the end of this chapter, we'll have a fully functional web app.

First, we should probably get a rough idea of what we want our app to look like. We've made it a surprisingly long way through this tutorial without figuring that out. We know we're building a JavaScript programming puzzle app, but we haven't decided how the puzzles will work or how the users should interact with them. It's time to give some thought to these issues and come up with a design.

Creating a View

User interface design can be one of the more challenging aspects of building an application. To build interfaces your users can navigate with ease, you need to understand the users' expectations and goals. It's hard to put yourself in their shoes and think about what they want, but if you have a partially working application in front of you, it can be a lot easier. What is already there inspires you, and what is missing grabs your attention.

 Just as a picture is worth a thousand words, a working prototype is worth a thousand meetings.

The problem view in our app will challenge users to "fill in the blank" to get a JavaScript function to return a truthy value. The problem, as presented to the users, should look something like this:

```
function problem() {
  return 2 + __ === 4;
}
```

Our users will try to figure out what JavaScript should be entered in place of the __ to make the problem() function return true. If they do that, the answer will be judged to be correct. This means each problem might have many different correct answers. To design this view, we need to think about the essential elements of this workflow.

This view is all about programming puzzles, so we'll need a way to present the problem. To provide a bit of context to our users, we'll want to show a title that includes the problem number. A description of the problem will help them understand exactly what they're supposed to do. To let them verify their answers, we'll need a way for users to enter the code that solves the problem. In this chapter, we're going to put all of these elements together to build our application's primary view. We'll add these elements to our view incrementally, checking our assumptions about the workflow along the way.

To improve our problem view, we'll first extract the markup for this view out to an *HTML template*. HTML templates are a great (and simple) way to manage markup. They're flexible, easily testable, and require no special libraries or tools. Using them is much easier than building the markup programmatically using jQuery, if for no other reason than we can use standard HTML editing tools and formatters to create it. Once we've created a template, we'll add a <title> element that we can use to show the title (rather than just appending text to the view). Before we can create this view template, we need to find a place for all the templates in our app to live.

To create a home for the application's templates, first create a new <div> in the app markup and give it the templates class. We'll use this element to hold all of our templates. Inside of that templates <div>, create another <div> with the problem-view class and add an <h3> element with the title class.

```
learnjs/3001/public/index.html
<body>
  <div class='markup'>
    <div class='view-container container'>
      <div class='landing-view'>
        <div class='row'>
          <div class='one-half column'>
            <h3>Learn JavaScript, one puzzle at a time.</h3>
            <a href='#problem-1' class='button button-primary'>Start Now!</a>
          </div>
          <div class='one-half column'>
            <img src='/images/HeroImage.jpg'/>
          </div>
        </div>
      </div>
➤     <div class='templates'>
➤       <div class='problem-view'>
➤         <h3 class='title'></h3>
➤       </div>
➤     </div>
    </div>
    <script type='text/javascript'>
      $(window).ready(learnjs.appOnReady);
    </script>
</body>
```

Next, you need to make a copy of this template in the problemView() function. Copying it lets you rebuild the view over and over again, without having to worry about state from one instance leaking into another. To do this, select the problem-view <div> out of the templates <div>, and use jQuery's clone() function to make a copy. You can see this clone operation in the updated version of our router figure on page 48.

Once you have that copy, you need to update the text for the <title> element. You can do this by selecting the <title> element with jQuery, then using the problem number to build the text for the title. Once that's done, return the view's markup from the view function. With all those changes, the problem view function should look like this:

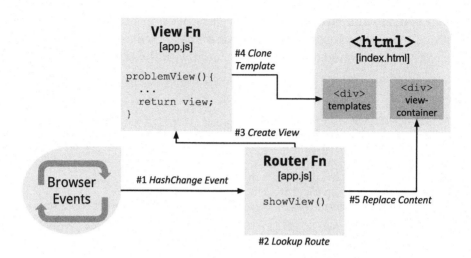

learnjs/3001/public/app.js

```
learnjs.problemView = function(problemNumber) {
  var view = $('.templates .problem-view').clone();
  view.find('.title').text('Problem #' + problemNumber);
  return view;
}
```

The last thing you'll need to do is to hide the templates <div> from the user. We don't want our templates showing up in the app, and you can hide them with a little bit of CSS. Add a rule to the inline <style> element in the <head> of index.html, like so:

learnjs/3001/public/index.html

```
<style type="text/css" media="all">
  body { margin-top: 30px; }
  .templates { display: none; }
</style>
```

Now, if you open the app and click the call to action button, it should switch to the problem view and show a simple title.

Problem #1

Using templates to create views like this makes it much easier to manage markup, while still keeping the application flexible and dynamic enough to show any content we like. jQuery makes it easy to clone, change, and append these templates without having to add a specific templating library, and as you'll see later, we can extend this technique to other parts of our application.

To build the rest of our problem view, we can add a description of the problem, the problem code itself, and a place for the users to provide an answer. Before we add any of that, however, we need to figure out where all this data is going to come from, and how we're going to make it available to our app. In short, we need a *data model*.

Joe asks:
Where'd the Tests Go?

While I think it extremely important to design for testability, and the best way to design for testability is to write tests first, this isn't a book about testing. So I'll continue to demonstrate tests that show a novel or advanced technique, but I'm going to spare you any tests that are similar to ones you've seen earlier in the book.

However, the rest of the code in this book is written test first. To do otherwise would leave you with an incomplete picture of how to build this kind of web application. It's one thing to design software that works for today; designing software that will continue to work as you change it is much more challenging. You can see all the tests (along with code) at pragprog.com.[a] If you have any questions about how a particular piece of code was tested, you'll find the answer there.

a.   https://pragprog.com/book/brapps/

Defining the Data Model

It's a common practice when building web applications to use object-oriented JavaScript[1] to define a data model. First, you create JavaScript classes (which are actually just functions) that use prototypical inheritance[2] to model your problem. You then create graphs of these objects in order to store your data and perform operations on it. If we were using that approach for this app, we'd probably wind up with Problem objects, which might have included a checkSolution function that accepted another object type (maybe Solution) as a parameter. Both of these object types might inherit persistence and serialization behavior from another object type (maybe Entity or Model).

With this app, we're going to take a different approach. Instead of defining a data model with a graph of JavaScript objects augmented with prototypical behavior, we're going to use vanilla data structures to store our data: just

---

1.   http://eloquentjavascript.net/06_object.html
2.   http://eloquentjavascript.net/06_object.html#h_SumMIRB7yn

arrays and objects. To manipulate this data, we're going to create a catalog of functions in the app to perform the operations we need.

By doing this, we hope to achieve low *object mapping impedance*. One of the limitations of object graph data models is that you have to map them back and forth to your underlying datastore. For example, if we were using a relational database for our app, then we might have to use an object-relational mapping (ORM) tool to serialize and deserialize our data to and from the database.

If we used a data model with prototypical inheritance, we might run into problems when we tried to serialize those objects. JavaScript objects make no real distinction between values and behavior. Functions are just properties on an object, like any other property such as a string or a number. If we mix data and behavior on the objects in our model, we'll have to separate them back out again when we go to serialize them to and from the database. Ideally, we'd like to have a more direct mapping from our model objects to the database, that doesn't require this step.

As you'll see in Chapter 5, *Storing Data in DynamoDB*, on page 93, the vanilla JavaScript data structure we'll use to hold both our problem data and the users' data will map directly into records stored in our database. DynamoDB supports storing JSON documents as individual records, so choosing a data model that can be serialized easily to JSON means we'll avoid having to do extra work to translate our data into a format that the database can understand. This is a great example of a situation where combining web standards with web services makes things much easier for us.

To get started, we'll create an array of objects to hold our problem data. Each object will contain the properties we need for each problem in the app. Define this array near the top of the app.js file (before the functions, but after the namespace). You can see the format of the objects in these two examples. Feel free to add more, if you like.

learnjs/3100/public/app.js

```
learnjs.problems = [
  {
    description: "What is truth?",
    code: "function problem() { return __; }"
  },
  {
    description: "Simple Math",
    code: "function problem() { return 42 === 6 * __; }"
  }
];
```

This data structure can easily evolve over time through refactoring. This is enough to start, and until we start persisting this data (or references to it), it will be easy to change our minds. Now that we have some data to work with, we can figure out how we're going to bind this data to the markup in our view. Then we'll be able to add more elements to the problem view—namely, the description and the code for the problem itself.

Data Binding

Now that we have our data model, we need to figure out a way to get this data into the markup. The most basic way is just to do what we did for the title: select the element that we want to populate, and set its content to be whatever it should be. This is fine for simple views, but if we have views that show a lot of data, writing code to populate every individual element can be tedious and error prone.

Another approach is to create an automatic mapping between the data in our data model and elements in the view's markup. This process is called *data binding*, and there are two kinds. With *one-way data binding*, data is inserted into the markup automatically. This is useful for read-only fields and other noneditable elements.

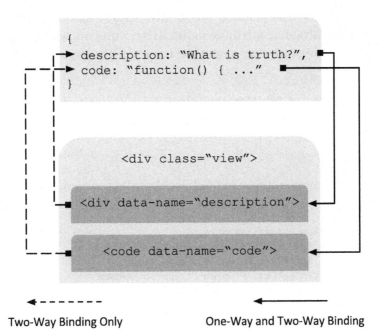

As the figure on page 51 shows, with *two-way data binding*, data can be inserted into the markup and then read back out into the model, typically when an event is triggered that signals the data was changed. This is generally used for user-editable data. For problem data, we're going to need a one-way data binding solution, which you can create using HTML5 *data attributes*.[3]

We can add data attributes to the elements in our view to specify what properties should be bound to those elements. It will then be easy to write a function that will apply the properties of a JavaScript object to an element. We need to add the new elements and their data attributes to our view:

learnjs/3200/public/index.html

```
<div class='templates'>
  <div class='problem-view'>
    <h3 class='title'></h3>
    <p data-name='description'></p>
    <pre><code data-name='code'></code></pre>
  </div>
</div>
```

Each data-name specifies the name of the property that should be bound to that element. Once you add these elements to the markup, you can create a data binding function named applyObject that takes a JavaScript object and updates the elements in a jQuery object based on the keys in the object. Using the attribute value CSS selector syntax with jQuery lets us easily select elements with a particular attribute value. Here, you can see how to build up that CSS selector expression using the names of the keys:

learnjs/3200/public/app.js

```
learnjs.applyObject = function(obj, elem) {
  for (var key in obj) {
    elem.find('[data-name="' + key + '"]').text(obj[key]);
  }
};
```

Use this in the problem view to bind problem data to elements in the view.

learnjs/3200/public/app.js

```
learnjs.problemView = function(data) {
  var problemNumber = parseInt(data, 10);
  var view = $('.templates .problem-view').clone();
  view.find('.title').text('Problem #' + problemNumber);
  learnjs.applyObject(learnjs.problems[problemNumber - 1], view);
  return view;
}
```

---

3. https://developer.mozilla.org/en-US/docs/Web/Guide/HTML/Using_data_attributes

> **Joe asks:**
> ## Why Not Use $.data()?
>
> You might be wondering why I'm not using jQuery's data function to read the data-name attributes in applyObject. The reason is that while jQuery's data function does allow you to access HTML5 data attributes, it maintains its own separate data object[a] in addition to the element's data attributes, and I don't want to get the two confused.
>
> _____
>
> a.   https://api.jquery.com/data/#data-html5

We now have a reusable function for one-way data binding. Of course, it has its limitations. It can only work with elements with text values, so it won't work on form elements like <input>, <select>, or <textarea>, but we don't need one-way data binding for those things right now. We may never need it, and if we do, we can add it later just as easily as we can add it now. This code is as simple as it can be for the present moment.

Now let's take a quick look at what we've done. If you navigate to the problem view, you should see this:

Problem #1

What is truth?

```
function problem() { return __; }
```

If you manually change the URL to #problem-2, the app should switch to the next problem. If that all works, we're ready to move on to the next step.

Growing the Data Model

We started this section by creating a simple data model—just an array with some objects in it. As our app grows, this will likely become more complex. We'll need to add new types of data, and persist that data to a database. As you build your own serverless applications, you'll likely need more than just an array to represent your data.

Rather than creating objects that have behavior, we should consider storing data in structures that we can manipulate easily using the JavaScript functions already available in the browser. Then we can build simple standalone functions that we can chain together to create complex behavior.

Let's say you created a function named formatCode that applied a formatter to the code in one of the question objects. To create a list of answer objects with formatted code, you could loop over the list and apply them one at a time.

learnjs/3913/public/tests/format_spec.js

```
var formattedProblems = [];
learnjs.problems.forEach(function(problem) {
  formattedProblems.push({
    code: learnjs.formatCode(problem.code),
    name: problem.name
  });
});
return formattedProblems;
```

However, if you're familiar with Array.map in JavaScript, you may have recognized that this code could be replaced easily. You just need to change formatCode to take one of the problem objects instead of just the text, and then we can shrink it down to this:

learnjs/3913/public/tests/format_spec.js

```
return learnjs.problems.map(learnjs.formatCode);
```

formatCode takes an object and returns a new object, so rather than just taking text and returning it, you can easily compose it with other functions. If you want a list of answer objects with formatted code and sorted by name, you can create a byName function to do the sort comparison, and then call

```
learnjs.problems.map(formatCode).sort(byName);
```

Building up a library of functions that all operate on the same kind of object, in lieu of an object hierarchy, lets us create a rich and expressive data model while still relying on the web standards that make data mapping easy. If we later decide, for example, to move our problem sets into a database instead of storing them directly in the application, none of our application logic will have to change, because the object will remain exactly the same.

Another challenge we'd like to avoid (or make as painless as possible) is that of *data migration*. Much of this pain can be mitigated by keeping static data in the app, as we've done with our problem sets. We can then deploy changes to the data schema and roll them back in tandem with the application logic.

For example, because users can't edit our problem list, we're able to store it right in the app. If we want to be able to reorder the list of problems while keeping the IDs consistent, we can replace our array indexes, which act as a sort of natural key, with regular primary keys. We can do this by introducing

Consider a Functional Library

Along with your own library of domain-specific functions you create for your data model, consider adding a library to your app to support a functional style, like Underscore.js[a] or Ramda[b] These libraries provide many functions beyond what the standard JavaScript Object and Array classes do, including things like pluck, groupBy, and union. You can even do true function composition, or create partially applied functions. When using this approach to data modeling, using a functional library can be an extremely valuable addition to your app.

a.   http://underscorejs.org/
b.   http://ramdajs.com/

a new field on the object, updating our app to search for problems by ID, and then deploying changes as an atomic operation by pushing everything to S3.

When building your own serverless single page apps, you'll likely find a lot of value in keeping your data model as simple and flexible as possible. Don't assume that you have to store data in a database—at least, not right away. You can always move it into the database later, so long as you don't pollute your data model with things that aren't data. The simple data structures that JavaScript provides are powerful enough to model many different types of problems, and easy to manipulate with tools that are within easy reach.

Looking for ways to avoid hard problems is usually the easiest way to solve them. Of course, that's not always possible. Once we start storing data in a database, these migrations will get a little trickier. We'll touch on that process in *Working with DynamoDB*, on page 93.

Now that we've defined a flexible data model, let's use it. In the next section, we're going to get some of this data on the screen so our users can see it. After that, we'll see how to provide visual feedback to users, and how to control navigation across different views.

Handling User Input

The original idea behind HTML <form> elements was to give web pages a way to send user-supplied data back to a server.[4] The form attributes action and method allow you to specify where and how to send this data when the user clicks the Submit button in the form. While we don't want to abandon the familiar look and feel of a form, we need a way to capture user input without

---

4.   https://developer.mozilla.org/en-US/docs/Web/Guide/HTML/Forms/Sending_and_retrieving_form_data

submitting a request to a server. We want our application to prevent the form submission and take action entirely in the browser.

Now that our app is presenting problems to the users, we're going to give the users a way to provide an answer. We'll want them to enter the code for their answer, hit a button to check it, and then see the results displayed somewhere. It should tell them whether they got it right or wrong, but it shouldn't provide any more information than that (no hints!). Although we're going to use HTML <form> elements to build this UI, we need to intercept any submit or click events that would cause the browser to try to post this data, and process the data in the app itself.

To support this part of the workflow, we need to add a <textarea> to our view. This element will provide enough space for our users to enter the code that defines their answer, which might be a few lines in some cases. We'll also need a button they can click to submit their answers, and some form of feedback that tells them whether the answer was correct.

To test this behavior, you'll have to simulate the user input. One way to do this is by setting the value of the <textarea> and then triggering a click event on the button using jQuery. By adding these tests to the problem view's describe section, you can create a reusable view variable created in that scope and initialized in a Jasmine beforeEach function. The following two tests reuse that view variable from the surrounding scope:

learnjs/3300/public/tests/app_spec.js

```javascript
describe('answer section', function() {
  it('can check a correct answer by hitting a button', function() {
    view.find('.answer').val('true');
    view.find('.check-btn').click();
    expect(view.find('.result').text()).toEqual('Correct!');
  });

  it('rejects an incorrect answer', function() {
    view.find('.answer').val('false');
    view.find('.check-btn').click();
    expect(view.find('.result').text()).toEqual('Incorrect!');
  });
});
```

To get these tests passing, you need the app to do something when users click that button. Unlike with the call to action button in the landing page, you'll need to handle this click programmatically, so you should add a click handler using jQuery. Returning false from the click handler will tell the browser not to submit the form. Submitting the form will cause the page to reload and the state of our application to reset, you want to avoid that.

learnjs/3300/public/app.js

```
learnjs.problemView = function(data) {
  var problemNumber = parseInt(data, 10);
  var view = $('.templates .problem-view').clone();
  var problemData = learnjs.problems[problemNumber - 1];
  var resultFlash = view.find('.result');

  function checkAnswer() {
    var answer = view.find('.answer').val();
    var test = problemData.code.replace('__', answer) + '; problem();';
    return eval(test);
  }

  function checkAnswerClick() {
    if (checkAnswer()) {
      resultFlash.text('Correct!');
    } else {
      resultFlash.text('Incorrect!');
    }
    return false;
  }

  view.find('.check-btn').click(checkAnswerClick);
  view.find('.title').text('Problem #' + problemNumber);
  learnjs.applyObject(problemData, view);
  return view;
}
```

Joe asks:
Isn't eval() Evil?

Why, yes. Yes, it is. In addition to just throwing an uncaught error if the user enters invalid JavaScript, as you'll see in *Sandboxing JavaScript Using Web Workers*, on page 142, using eval() like this makes our app vulnerable to a particular kind of Cross-Site Scripting (XSS) attack. For example, if someone were able to trick a user into entering arbitrary JavaScript as their solution to a problem, all kinds of bad things could happen. Later, you'll see a way to evaluate JavaScript safely, inside of a "sandbox" that's isolated from the rest of our application. For now, the risks are low enough to deal with.

In addition to the click handler, the checkAnswer() function on line 7 will let you validate a user's answer and determine if it is correct. This function builds up a JavaScript string that checks for a truthy return value, and then calls eval() on it to get the result.

Once you've created the click handler, add the new markup to the problem view template. You'll need that <textarea>, along with a button to click, and a flash element to use to show the result. The flash element can be just about anything. For now, just make it a <p>. Adding the u-full-width class from Skeleton will make the <textarea> wide enough to use comfortably. You'll also want to add a class to style it with a more code-friendly font. Finally, because these are all form elements, you'll want to put them in a <form>.

learnjs/3300/public/index.html

```
<div class='templates'>
  <div class='problem-view'>
    <h3 class='title'></h3>
    <p data-name='description'></p>
    <pre><code data-name='code'></code></pre>
    <form>
      <textarea class='u-full-width answer'></textarea>
      <div>
        <button class='button-primary check-btn'>Check Answer</button>
        <p class='result'></p>
      </div>
    </form>
  </div>
</div>
```

If the tests go into an infinite reload loop after adding this markup, check that you added the return false statement to the button click handler. What's happening here is that the button click is attempting to submit the form, which reloads the page, which runs the test, which submits the form...

If your tests *don't* go into an infinite reload loop, it might be because they're passing! Yay! If so, switch back to the browser tab where you had the app running, and take a look.

Problem #1

What is truth?

```
function problem() { return __; }
```

```
true
```

CHECK ANSWER

Correct!

This works. It's a little plain, but it works. We want to get the workflow correct before we start spending time improving the layout, and there's something about this view's workflow that still needs our attention. If we enter an incorrect answer (like false) and then a different incorrect answer (like 1 == 2), the view doesn't change at all. We'll want to do something about that next.

Using Visual Feedback Effectively

In a traditional web application, when users take an action, it is usually followed by a page load. While not an ideal user experience, it is familiar, and it provides a crucial bit of feedback: acknowledgment that users did something that requires an action. Giving users this kind of feedback is an essential part of building a functional single page web app.

The problem view lacks this feedback right now. Unless the answer they enter actually changes whether our solution is correct or incorrect, there's no feedback to tell users that the app has actually responded and checked the answer. Imagine someone who *thinks* they have a correct answer, but the answer has a small typo. The user might click the Check Answer button over and over again, thinking that our app is just broken, when it's actually checking the answer every time. We can fix this problem by providing some visual feedback, and we'll do this using the jQuery Effects API.

The jQuery Effects API has a number of different functions[5] for generating effects. These functions are quite often the most abused in all of web development. Needlessly flashing, moving, expanding, or shrinking elements can disorient and annoy users. Using these effects to provide subtle feedback, however, can give our users assurance that our app is working as they expect.

In our case, we're going to use the fadeOut and fadeIn effects to let users know when we've reevaluated their answer. To do this, you can create a new function in the application namespace called flashElement.

learnjs/3400/public/app.js

```
learnjs.flashElement = function(elem, content) {
  elem.fadeOut('fast', function() {
    elem.html(content);
    elem.fadeIn();
  });
}
```

---

5. http://api.jquery.com/category/effects/

We can use this function from the problem view, but we can also reuse it in any view that needs a visual effect, like this:

learnjs/3400/public/app.js

```
Line 1  function checkAnswerClick() {
          if (checkAnswer()) {
            learnjs.flashElement(resultFlash, 'Correct!');
          } else {
            learnjs.flashElement(resultFlash, 'Incorrect!');
     10   }
          return false;
        }
```

In addition to the 'fast' string specifying how quickly the animation runs, the fadeOut function takes a callback that is invoked when the effect is complete. You can use that callback to trigger the change of content and fade in. The effect from a user's point of view will be that the existing content fades out, and the new content fades in, giving them feedback that lets them know their answer was understood.

Now if you load up the app and enter an answer, you should get a quick but clearly visible flash every time we check the answer. This gives our users assurance that our app did what they expected, even if the state of their results does not change.

Controlling Navigation

Traditional web applications often control navigation through a combination of view and controller code. Typically, this is done by rendering links directly into views, by adding routes that conditionally redirect to other routes, or by adding controllers that render different views, depending on the application state. In our app, we'll only use one function for doing this. We don't have distinct controllers, so the responsibility for controlling navigation falls to the view functions. When rendering a view, they need to either add links to other views or add behavior that can cause the browser to navigate somewhere else.

At this point, our app lets users view and solve the first problem. That's good, but we need to guide our users to the next problem in a way that keeps them engaged. To do this, we're going to enhance the problem view function to generate a link to the next problem. This link will only appear when the current problem is solved.

To create this link, we're going to make a template. Up until now, we've only been using templates for views, but we can use them for any bit of markup that we need to create. Just add a <div> to the templates <div> like this:

learnjs/3500/public/index.html

```
<div class='correct-flash'>
  <span>Correct!</span> <a>Next Problem</a>
</div>
```

Now that we have a template we want to use, we'll need to clone it. There's no sense in duplicating that code all over the place, so start by extracting a new function from the problemView function.

learnjs/3500/public/app.js

```
learnjs.template = function(name) {
  return $('.templates .' + name).clone();
}
```

This template function will come in handy whenever you create a template, whether it's for a view or just a bit of markup like our link. Lastly, you'll need to update the click handler for the Check Answer button. Clone the template and then update the href attribute to point to the next problem.

learnjs/3500/public/app.js

```
function checkAnswerClick() {
  if (checkAnswer()) {
    var correctFlash = learnjs.template('correct-flash');
    correctFlash.find('a').attr('href', '#problem-' + (problemNumber + 1));
    learnjs.flashElement(resultFlash, correctFlash);
  } else {
    learnjs.flashElement(resultFlash, 'Incorrect!');
  }
  return false;
}
```

Creating links dynamically like this is one way our view functions can control how users navigate through our app. If we wanted to, we could also have the app make the decision about where to go right when the button is clicked. By setting the window.location.hash property in the checkAnswerClick click handler, we could redirect users to any view using JavaScript to control the logic. For example, in the case of an incorrect answer, if we wanted to provide a different help link depending on the type of answer users provided, we could easily do that in the click handler.

Using our shiny new template function, we can expand the use of templates to create HTML component functions. These functions encapsulate the creation and initialization of a template and can be a great way to make behavior more testable, or share components between views. For example, to handle the case of the last problem in our list, we'll probably want to redirect users somewhere else. Sending them back to the landing page seems like a decent approach, so let's do that. Before you write the tests for that behavior, extract a function named buildCorrectFlash from the answer button click handler, and then test the function directly. When you're done, you should get something that looks like this:

learnjs/3700/public/app.js

```
learnjs.buildCorrectFlash = function (problemNum) {
  var correctFlash = learnjs.template('correct-flash');
  var link = correctFlash.find('a');
  if (problemNum < learnjs.problems.length) {
    link.attr('href', '#problem-' + (problemNum + 1));
  } else {
    link.attr('href', '');
    link.text("You're Finished!");
  }
  return correctFlash;
}
```

Pulling this behavior out into a separate function not only makes it easier to test, but it also makes the view behavior easier to test, because it creates a testing seam that can be easily mocked out with a spy. Now that we have users navigating through our app, we're ready to create another essential part of any single page app: the application shell.

Creating an Application Shell

When using the app, you may have noticed that reloading the problem view can sometimes cause the landing page markup to temporarily flash onto the screen. This flash of markup occurs when the browser renders the page once before triggering the event that loads the application. This can occur, or not, depending on exactly how quickly the various resources of the application are loaded.

This flash of markup is annoying at best, and confusing at worst. Clearly, this is something we're going to want to address. The good news is that it's a pretty simple fix, and the change will create a new and important structure in our application: the *shell*.

The shell is the visible markup that's outside the templates and the view container. Anything in the shell will be visible in every view. We can use the shell to add things like navigation bars, logos, sidebars, or menus to the app. We can also use it as a parent for fixed-position elements that should be available in any view, like chat windows, tooltips, or dialogs.

Extracting the Landing Page

To create the shell, first move the landing-view <div> from the view-container into the templates <div>.

learnjs/3800/public/index.html

```
<div class='markup'>
  <div class='view-container container'>
  </div>
  <div class='templates'>
    <div class='landing-view'>
    <!-- Markup Continues... -->
```

This should cause a test to fail. To get it passing again, you need to create a view function for the landing view.

learnjs/3800/public/app.js

```
learnjs.landingView = function() {
  return learnjs.template('landing-view');
}
```

Then add the view function to the routes object.

learnjs/3800/public/app.js

```
var routes = {
  '#problem': learnjs.problemView,
  '': learnjs.landingView
};
```

With that, the tests should be passing again. Creating an application shell has also fixed another problem: the back button is working! If you click the call to action button and then hit the back button in your browser, you should return to the landing page. If you want to, you can create alias routes that map to this view, like "#landing" or simply "#". Just add another entry to the routes object that maps that route to the learnjs.landingView function.

Adding a Toolbar

Now that we've extracted all of our content out into views and created an application shell, let's add something to it. A simple toolbar would be a good addition to our app. Start by adding a <div> containing an unordered list to the markup, just above the view container.

learnjs/3901/public/index.html

```
<div class='nav-container no-select fixed-top u-full-width'>
  <ul class='inline-list hover-links nav-list six columns'>
    <li><a class='text-lg' href="#">LearnJS</a></li>
    <li><a href="#problem-1">Start</a></li>
  </ul>
</div>
<div class='view-container container'>
</div>
```

This unordered list will become our navbar, once we style it appropriately. As you can see in this example, you can add list items with anchors to create links into the app. Here, we've created two links that map to routes in our app: one back to the landing page, and one to the problem view.

To style these elements, we're going to add some classes. Skeleton CSS boilerplate gives us the u-full-width class, which ensures this navbar spans the width of the page. The six and columns classes keep the list of links in the left half of the navbar (the first six of twelve columns), creating space on the right side for other elements.

For the classes that apply our custom CSS rules, we want to organize and name our classes around the style they create, rather than using names that describe or depend on the structure of the markup. For example, to display our list inline, we can use the class inline-list.

learnjs/3901/public/index.html

```
.inline-list {
  margin-bottom: 0px; /* Skeleton reset */
}
.inline-list li {
  display: inline;
  margin: 0 20px 0 0;
}
```

We want this navbar to be fixed to the top of the screen, so it's visible even if the user scrolls down the page. To do this, you can create a rule for the class fixed-top that positions the navbar at the top of the page, and with a high enough z-index to be above the rest of the content. You'll also need to change the margin-top property in the body CSS rule from 30px to 60px, to account for the new height of the navbar.

learnjs/3901/public/index.html

```
.fixed-top {
  position: fixed;
  top: 0px;
  z-index: 1024;
}
```

You can prevent users from accidentally selecting the navbar elements instead of clicking them by using the user-select property. Not all browsers fully support this yet, so you have to use *vendor prefixes* in addition to the standard CSS property name.

learnjs/3901/public/index.html

```
.no-select {
  user-select: none;
  -webkit-user-select: none;
  -ms-user-select: none;
  -moz-user-select: none;
}
```

Vendor Prefixes

Vendor prefixes are a convention used by browser manufacturers to add experimental CSS features to their browsers before a web standard is approved and adopted. Although the user-select CSS property is supported in many browsers, it is not yet part of any World Wide Web Consortium (W3C) CSS specification, so using multiple properties with the appropriate vendor prefix helps ensure our app works the same way across different browsers.

Although we use links in our navbar, we don't want to always have them be underlined like normal links. Instead, we're going to apply a style when users hover over the links. We could use a shadow or other CSS effect, but for this app, we'll keep it simple by just doing an underline. You can do this by creating a rule for the hover-links class like so:

learnjs/3901/public/index.html

```
.hover-links a { text-decoration: none; }
.hover-links a:hover { text-decoration: underline; }
```

We need to set the color, size, and padding on our toolbar so that it takes up the entire width of the screen like a normal toolbar would. To do this, create a rule for the nav-container class.

learnjs/3901/public/index.html

```
.nav-container {
  padding-left: 40px;
  background: #666;
}
.nav-container a { color: white; }
```

Lastly, if you haven't already, add an alias route for the landing view, like the one we used in our first navbar link.

learnjs/3901/public/app.js

```
var routes = {
  '#problem': learnjs.problemView,
  '#': learnjs.landingView,
  '': learnjs.landingView
};
```

Once you're done adding these rules and elements, you should have a navbar that looks like this:

Now that we have an application shell, complete with a toolbar, there's more to our app than just a bunch of views. Next, we'll need to figure out a way to tie all the parts of our app together.

Using Custom Events

Right now, it's easy for our views to invoke behavior in the rest of the application. Our data model functions, for example, are easily shared among the views. One thing that's missing is a way for the app to trigger behavior in the views. There's no good way for the app to reach into the scope of the view functions to make things happen.

One approach we could take is to add a button to our shiny new toolbar and have each view register a click handler when it is created. However, without a mechanism to remove that click handler, that handler and any variables in its scope will never be garbage collected. As users move through the views, our memory usage would gradually increase until the application crashes.

Semantic CSS Classes

I didn't explain what each of the individual CSS properties do in this example, figuring that the Internet could probably do a more thorough job. However, you should hopefully be able to understand the intent behind each rule from the class names. Rather than just putting a single class name on an element and styling it using that class, I like to break up rules into semantic names that are as focused as possible. Not only does this make the code easier to understand, but it also makes it more likely that I can reuse these classes elsewhere.

To avoid this problem, we can use a *custom event* to send messages to our views. This can be useful when the current view may or may not need to take action to respond to some other bit of behavior in our application, such as removing event handlers when the view is replaced. By having the view register an event listener, we can trigger behavior in the views without having to break the encapsulation provided by the view function or create memory leaks that destabilize the app.

One thing we need to figure out when adding these events is who is going to trigger them. In this case, the router knows when it's about to replace the current view with another view. Sometimes, a view will hold on to resources that it needs to release when the view is replaced. Subscribing to an event gives the view a mechanism to do just that.

Instead of a library or framework to manage these events, we're going to rely on web standards to act as the foundation, and we're going to build a few functions on top of it that are specific to our app. At this point in the book, this approach should fill you with a certain sense of deja vu.

Specifically, we're going to use the event system already provided by the Document Object Model (DOM), and trigger custom events that our views can listen to. DOM events are triggered on element, and they bubble up the element hierarchy. We can send events to views by triggering an event on every child of the view-container element (which should only be the view). The view can then subscribe to those events by binding an event listener to the element that it returns as the view. To trigger these kinds of events, you can make a new function in the learnjs namespace:

learnjs/3912/public/app.js

```
learnjs.triggerEvent = function(name, args) {
  $('.view-container>*').trigger(name, args);
}
```

Taking advantage of the new event mechanism, we can add a Skip button for
the problem view to the navbar. This button lets users skip to the next problem, even if they haven't solved the current one. This button only shows up
when the problem view is loaded, and it is removed when the problem view
is removed.

To be able to act when a view is removed, you have to trigger an event when
that happens. That requires a change to the router function. Before the view
is replaced, you can trigger the event letting any existing views know they're
being removed. You can do this in the showView() function, after the new view
has been created, with the following code:

learnjs/3912/public/app.js

```
learnjs.triggerEvent('removingView', []);
$('.view-container').empty().append(viewFn(hashParts[1]));
```

Now, you just need to make the changes to the problem view to add and
remove the buttons. First, you'll need to add the necessary behavior to the
problemView() function. The following code should do the trick, once you've
added the necessary markup for the skip-btn (we'll do that next). Don't forget
to check if we're at the end of the problem list. Also, note the use of jQuery's
bind function to attach an event listener to the view element.

learnjs/3912/public/app.js

```
if (problemNumber < learnjs.problems.length) {
  var buttonItem = learnjs.template('skip-btn');
  buttonItem.find('a').attr('href', '#problem-' + (problemNumber + 1));
  $('.nav-list').append(buttonItem);
  view.bind('removingView', function() {
    buttonItem.remove();
  });
}
```

Next, we need to make a couple of changes to the markup. First, create a
template for the button. You can add this to the templates <div> you created
earlier.

learnjs/3912/public/index.html

```
<li class='skip-btn'>
  <a>Skip This Problem</a>
</li>
```

With that, we should have a working Skip button. If you navigate to the problem view and then back to the landing page, you should see that the button disappears. Removing the view from the DOM using jQuery's empty function, as we do, cleans up associated data and event handlers. So you don't have to worry about cleaning up the cleanup function.

Now that we have this event system in place, we can use it for lots of different things. Once we start talking to web services, we could use events to inform views that data in our model has been updated, or that users have taken actions such as logging in or out. For now, we're happy to use it for cleaning up references and preventing a memory leak. It's time to deploy a new version of the app.

Deploy Again

Now that our application is functional, we're ready to deploy again. Users can now view and solve JavaScript puzzles, and they can navigate from one problem to the next. In this chapter, we only added a few puzzles to our problem list, but you can easily add more if you like. Try to think of some easy ones to start, then throw in some real brain teasers, just to make things interesting!

Next Steps

Now that you know how to quickly and iteratively build web interfaces, here are some other topics you might want to investigate before moving on to the next chapter.

Web Accessibility

Not everyone who tries to use the app is going to use a mainstream browser. Visually impaired users are going to be using a *screen reader*, which offers a very different kind of experience. Many web developers who try using a screen reader for the first time find the experience to be shockingly frustrating.

Designing accessible web applications is a deep topic, well beyond the scope of this book, but it would be irresponsible of me not to inform you of the basics. Here are some great resources for creating accessible apps:

http://www.w3.org/standards/webdesign/accessibility

http://itstiredinhere.com/accessibility

Creating a Home Screen Icon

Many mobile devices support adding links to web applications as home screen buttons. These links appear right alongside native applications, even allowing you to specify an icon to represent them. The techniques for doing this are, unfortunately, vendor specific. However, adding the necessary meta elements to your app for the more popular vendors can be a great way to connect with your users.

iOS: https://developer.apple.com/library/ios/documentation/AppleApplications/Reference/ SafariWebContent/ConfiguringWebApplications/ConfiguringWebApplications.html

Chrome for Android: https://developer.chrome.com/multidevice/android/installtohome-screen

CSS Animations

We covered how to use jQuery effects to provide visual feedback, but they're not the only, or even the most common, way of doing so. CSS 3 animations[6] are a powerful way to achieve the same kinds of effects. Browser support can be limited for certain features, but it is generally well supported.

Form Validation

The process we used to check the answer for our problem view is usually referred to as *form validation*. While the validation in this app is highly specialized, you can find libraries that will perform more conventional forms of validation for you, such as validate.js and Parse.ly.

In the next chapter, we're going to add the first of many web services to our application. We'll introduce user identities and connect our application to social media accounts provided by vendors such as Google and Facebook. However, instead of building our own system for storing passwords and other sensitive user data, we're going to get Amazon to do it for us.

---

6.   https://developer.mozilla.org/en-US/docs/Web/CSS/animation

CHAPTER 4

Identity as a Service with Amazon Cognito

Identity is an essential concept in most applications. Any software that collects data from users must have some way to organize, access, and secure that data. In a traditional web app, the application server often manages identity through the use of browser cookies. Because of the rules that browsers enforce, cookies from different origins[1] are not shared. This means that if you have an application server that manages identity tokens using cookies, then all your other web services must share the same origin in order to access that cookie and authenticate the request.

However, if you treat identity management as just another web service, you can separate a lot of these concerns. Security credentials managed at the application layer (in JavaScript) don't have to worry about the same origin policy. That means you can use a wide array of services directly from the browser, without an intermediary holding all the keys and acting as a proxy.

With a serverless app, you can shift responsibility for managing identity to a third-party web service...along with all of the headaches and risks that go with it. Having a secure web service that can manage identities and provide authorization for other web services completely changes the way we can build web applications. One such identity management service is Amazon Cognito.

Amazon's Cognito service allows us to manage identity through *identity federation*. This means that we can use identities from a variety of *identity providers* (such as Google, Facebook, or even our own app) and link them with a single identity record provided by Cognito. Cognito stores these records in what it calls an *identity pool*. Amazon's IAM console lets us define policies that grant users in this identity pool access to any of Amazon's web services based on a number of different criteria. This allows our application to make

---

1. https://developer.mozilla.org/en-US/docs/Web/Security/Same-origin_policy

requests on behalf of an authenticated user—right from the browser—without having to route our requests through an application server. Authorization then becomes a concern of the infrastructure, rather than of the app.

With a traditional web application, identity information like this would normally be stored in the database. You'd have a table of users, and you'd probably use the primary key from the rows in that table to join with records in other tables. If you know what you're doing, this record would include properly salted and hashed passwords. If the phrase "properly salted and hashed" sounds like directions out of a cookbook to you, then Cognito is your godsend. Instead of managing our own user records, we'll use the identifier that Cognito creates, and we'll include it in any records we write to the database. By using Cognito, we can not only avoid having to manage all of that infrastructure, but we'll also avoid the security concerns inherent in managing other people's passwords.

In this chapter, we'll see how to manage identity without requiring an application server that holds all the keys. To enable social logins to our app, we'll create an *identity pool* to act as a repository for our user identities. We'll connect our app with third-party *identity providers* such as Google and Facebook. Then we'll create profiles that will let our app directly access any Amazon web service right from the browser. After that, we'll be able to take the next step: storing user data in a database.

Connecting to External Identity Providers

The identity access systems created by Google, Facebook, and other providers are (somewhat loosely) based on the OAuth2 standard, which allows web apps and other clients to gain temporary access to information via HTTP. While the standard itself has some serious problems,[2] the implementations created by the major vendors are well understood at this point, and offer many integration opportunities.

Using Cognito to manage these interactions for us means we can avoid some of the problems of OAuth2 while still taking advantage of the benefits. First, we'll need to get a unique identifier from the identity provider. Each provider has its own method for doing this. Once we've got that ID, however, we can associate it with a Cognito identity, and then use that Cognito identity to get AWS credentials.

---

2.   http://hueniverse.com/2012/07/26/oauth-2-0-and-the-road-to-hell/

Cognito is not available in some AWS availability zones.

Putting all these pieces together, we can see how users connect to our application. First, they log in with a third-party identity provider. This login process may involve entering a username and password on the provider's site, as well as on a confirmation screen.

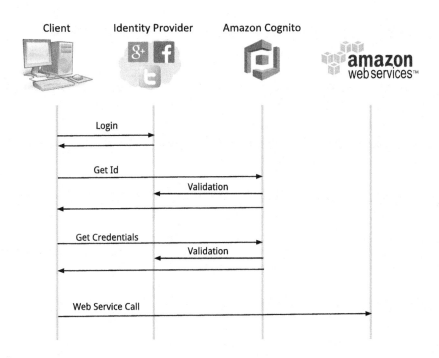

Once that's complete, our app can take the provider's ID token and send it to Cognito along with our identity pool ID. Cognito uses the token to connect back to the identity provider to confirm the user's identity. Cognito then associates the third-party identity with a new Cognito identity, and it adds the Cognito identity to the identity pool. Cognito then returns the identity information, which we can use later to request temporary AWS credentials. Cognito can refresh these credentials automatically if the provider ID token is still valid. The app uses those AWS credentials to make web service requests to any service authorized by our identity pool's authenticated user profile.

Google is the first identity provider we're going to add to our app, but you can use a similar process to add support for other providers. To get a Google ID that we can send to Cognito, Google requires that we follow a process called Google+ Sign-in.[3] The first step in this process is creating and configuring a Google project in the Google Developers Console (also called the Google API console). To do that, we need to follow these steps:

1. Open Google Developers Console[4] and log in using your Google account.

2. Click the Create Project button (it may be in a drop-down in the navbar).

3. Give your project a name.

4. After the project is generated, open the project detail page and select Enable and Manage APIs under Use Google APIs in the dashboard.

5. Find the Google+ API and enable it.

6. Select Credentials in the left sidebar.

7. Click the tab that says "OAuth consent screen" and fill out the form presented. This information will be presented to users when they are asked to connect to your app with Google. For now, you only need a product name, but you can add as much as you like.

8. Click the Add Credentials button and select "OAuth 2.0 client ID."

9. Select "Web application" as the application type, and click Create.

After that, you'll be presented with a form like this:

---

3.   https://developers.google.com/identity/sign-in/web/sign-in
4.   http://console.developers.google.com

On this screen, you'll need to add all the *origins* we expect our app to be running from. When authorizing our application, Google will expect the request to be made from an app running on one of these locations. It verifies this using the origin header [5] added by the browser before it makes the request. If the request comes from anywhere else, it will be denied.

Cognito User Pools

In addition to third-party identity providers like Google and Facebook, Cognito provides a mechanism to create user accounts that are specific to your app. These accounts are not associated with a third-party identity and are authenticated using a password. These kinds of accounts can be managed with a Cognito *user pool*.

User pools contains records of individual users, and can act as a source of identity for identity pools. User pools manage their own authentication credentials and let you specify additional attributes to associate with each user, such as an email address, phone number, birth date, or username. You can configure your user pool to require passwords of a certain strength and email/SMS verification for new users. You can even permit users to authenticate with multifactor authentication, or require it if the app contains particularly sensitive information.

User pools can be a way to take advantage of the serverless benefits of Cognito while still providing a dedicated login for your app that feels familiar to users who don't want to use social logins. Although as of this writing user pools are still in beta, the feature is expected to be ready for production use in the summer of 2016. If you don't want to use social logins for your apps, Cognito user pools might be a great alternative.

 If you're using a different development web server, ensure the port numbers for the localhost URLs are correct.

Once the project is created, we need to copy the Client ID at the top of this page. We can safely ignore the Client secret. The Client ID should look something like this:

```
351607165455-uesp1702cesp44vbn539m7rm6gg5ov3h.apps.googleusercontent.com
```

Now that we've created an application in the Google Developers Console, we can use the application's Client ID to connect our app with Google. Next, we need to create an identity pool in the Cognito AWS console.

---

5. https://developer.mozilla.org/en-US/docs/Glossary/Origin

Creating an Identity Pool

An identity pool is the container we'll use to hold all the user identities in our application. Sort of like a Users table in a database, it holds the list of users, and it shows what credentials they used to connect. Creating one is fairly straightforward, but understanding how it works requires a deeper dive into Amazon IAM.

Identities in an identity pool can be authenticated (using an identity provider), or they can be unauthenticated, meaning that they're essentially anonymous. You can reuse identity pools across applications, which will let your users share data between them. Amazon sets a limit of sixty identity pools active at one time, but there is no limit to the number of identities (users) you can have in a pool.

Identity Pool Configuration

To create the identity pool, you can use the sspa script in the prepared workspace. The create_pool action creates a new identity pool, along with all the associated IAM configuration, based on a configuration directory you specify. In the prepared workspace, open the directory conf/cognito/identity_pools/learnjs. Open the file config.json and take a look:

learnjs/4001/conf/cognito/identity_pools/learnjs/config.json

```
{
    "AllowUnauthenticatedIdentities": false,
    "SupportedLoginProviders": {
        "accounts.google.com": "<Google Client ID Here!>"
    }
}
```

Once you add the Google Client ID to this configuration, it will contain all the information the sspa script needs to create a new identity pool. The AllowUnauthenticatedIdentities property specifies whether or not Cognito users in this pool must authenticate with an identity provider. While we won't require all our users to sign in to use the app, we will require them to sign in if they want to save their answers.

The SupportedLoginProviders lists the identity providers we want to support, along with the IDs Cognito should use to verify their tokens. If you want to add additional identity providers, you can do that here before creating the pool. Once you're ready, run this command:

```
learnjs $ ./sspa create_pool conf/cognito/identity_pools/learnjs
```

The sspa script uses the AWS CLI tool you set up in Chapter 1, and the configuration in a directory you specify, to create a new identity pool. The name of the pool will be the same as the configuration directory itself. If you want to create an additional identity pool, you can make a new directory, add a config.json file (which can just be a symlink), and run the command again. This can be useful when creating a test environment.

After running the command, some additional files will show up in the configuration directory. Let's go through them one at a time, so that you understand what the sspa script is doing for you.

The first file that's created is pool_info.json. This file contains information returned from the Cognito service after the pool was created. As you can see here, in addition to the information that was in the config.json file, you'll find the identity pool's ID.

learnjs/4001/conf/cognito/identity_pools/learnjs/pool_info.json

```
{
  "IdentityPoolId": "us-east-1:71958f90-67bf-4571-aa17-6e4c1dfcb67d",
  "AllowUnauthenticatedIdentities": false,
  "SupportedLoginProviders": {
    "accounts.google.com":
      "ABC123ADDYOURID.apps.googleusercontent.com"
  },
  "IdentityPoolName": "learnjs"
}
```

In addition to creating the identity pool itself, the script generated some other resources for our app. Before we look at those, we need to take a minute to understand how a user gains access to web services using an identity pool.

IAM Roles and Policies

One reason we use a Cognito identity pool in our app is that it allows our users to easily assume IAM *roles*. A role works a lot like an IAM user, in that it can use policies that specify what actions can and can't be performed with the role. Unlike users, roles are intended to be used by many different people, and users can assume roles in order to perform certain actions. To let our users access the services that our app requires, we need to grant them permission to do so. Creating a role for the authenticated users in our identity pool is one way to do that.

For a user to assume a role, you have to create a policy that allows it. When creating the role, you need to include this policy, called an *assumed role policy*. Note that this policy is separate from any policies that grant the user permission to access services (like reading from a DynamoDB table). The sspa script defines this assumed role policy in a file named assume_role_policy.json, which is added to the identity pool configuration directory. It should look something like this:

learnjs/4001/conf/cognito/identity_pools/learnjs/assume_role_policy.json

```
{
  "Version": "2012-10-17",
  "Statement": [
    {
      "Sid": "",
      "Effect": "Allow",
      "Principal": {
        "Federated": "cognito-identity.amazonaws.com"
      },
      "Action": "sts:AssumeRoleWithWebIdentity",
      "Condition": {
        "StringEquals": {
          "cognito-identity.amazonaws.com:aud":
            "us-east-1:71958f90-67bf-4571-aa17-6e4c1dfcb67d"
        },
        "ForAnyValue:StringLike": {
          "cognito-identity.amazonaws.com:amr": "authenticated"
        }
      }
    }
  ]
}
```

We touched on IAM policies in the first chapter, when we set up AWS CLI for the first time. You can add additional policies to roles or users to grant access to services. The policy we used in Chapter 1 was a managed policy named AdministratorAccess. The policy we used previously is a *custom policy*. Custom policies give you fine-grained control over access to specific resources, grant access to specific types of users, or otherwise limit or expand the access granted based on some conditions. Let's take a look at some of the properties in this policy document and see what they do.

The Effect entry in the policy's sole statement specifies that it grants access to an action (rather than revoking it). The Action section specifies that this policy should grant permission to use the sts:AssumeRoleWithWebIdentity action. Cognito uses Amazon's Security Token Service (STS) to generate temporary AWS credentials for our users. The AssumeRoleWithWebIdentity action lets a user who has authenticated with an identity provider assume this role and get those generated credentials.

The Condition entry in a policy is used to control fine-grained access by requiring that any of the operations defined in the statement be on items where the hash value portion of the key matches the value defined. The first Condition clause in this policy restricts the use of this role to just one identity pool, which is identified by the pool ID. The other clause in the Condition restricts the role to only authenticated Cognito users. If you wanted to allow unauthenticated users to access AWS services, you would typically create a separate role with its own assumed role policy.

The sspa script uses this policy to create a new role. You can see the response from AWS in role_info.json:

learnjs/4001/conf/cognito/identity_pools/learnjs/role_info.json

```json
{
  "Role": {
    "AssumeRolePolicyDocument": {
      "Version": "2012-10-17",
      "Statement": [
        {
          "Action": "sts:AssumeRoleWithWebIdentity",
          "Principal": {
            "Federated": "cognito-identity.amazonaws.com"
          },
          "Effect": "Allow",
          "Condition": {
            "StringEquals": {
              "cognito-identity.amazonaws.com:aud":
                "us-east-1:71958f90-67bf-4571-aa17-6e4c1dfcb67d"
            },
            "ForAnyValue:StringLike": {
              "cognito-identity.amazonaws.com:amr": "authenticated"
            }
          },
          "Sid": ""
        }
      ]
    },
    "RoleId": "AROAJ5QOAOJOWUAORXS3S",
    "CreateDate": "2015-12-11T02:23:13.981Z",
    "RoleName": "learnjs_cognito_authenticated",
    "Path": "/",
    "Arn": "arn:aws:iam::730171000947:role/learnjs_cognito_authenticated"
  }
}
```

Aside from the AssumeRolePolicyDocument we've already discussed, you can see other information about the role in this response, including the name, the *Amazon Resource Name* (ARN), and the date it was created.

You can view your newly created identity pool in the Cognito AWS web console.

With that, the identity pool is created. We're now ready to integrate Cognito identities into the app. To do this, we're going to add a button to our navbar that will let users connect using their Google accounts. We'll also add a new view that will let users verify what information we have about them.

Fetching a Google Identity

One of the differences with an app that uses an identity provider is that users don't log in—at least, not in the traditional sense. Because we're federating identities through Cognito, users can connect to our application through an identity provider, and we never have to deal with reading or storing passwords. For that reason, we don't need a login page, but we do need a way for users to connect using whatever identity they might want to use. For now, we're just going to continue working with Google identities, but you can add more for your users if you like using a similar process.

We've already created an application in the Google Developers Console and linked it to our identity pool. Now we need to build the actual mechanism that lets users connect with our app. As you saw previously, this process is called Google+ Sign-in. We need to add a Sign-In button in the navbar of our app to give users something to click when they want to connect.

You might find Google's process for adding a Sign-In button a bit...intrusive. Rather than making an API call, we need to let Google insert the button into our markup. Do this by loading and configuring a JavaScript library provided, and creating a <div> on our page that acts as a container for the button.

To load this library, we need to add two tags to our page's <head> element. First, we need to add a <script> element to pull in the Google JavaScript API (gapi). Per Google's recommendation, this element includes the async and defer properties, which tell the browser not to pause HTML parsing while fetching this script, and to execute the script after the parsing is complete.

learnjs/4000/public/index.html

```
<script src="https://apis.google.com/js/platform.js" async defer></script>
```

Next, configure this library by adding some metadata to identify the Google project you created. Using the same Client ID you entered in the identity pool configuration page, create a <meta> element in the <head> of the page like this:

```
<meta name="google-signin-client_id"
  content="ABC123ADDYOURID.apps.googleusercontent.com" />
```

Once you've added these, define a function that the Google API will use as a callback. It will be invoked when the user has connected successfully. Name the callback function googleSignIn, at Google's suggestion. Note that this function cannot live in the learnjs namespace. For now, create the function and log the arguments to the console, so you can confirm that it's being invoked.

learnjs/4000/public/app.js

```
function googleSignIn() {
  console.log(arguments);
}
```

Now that you've configured the required JavaScript library and added a callback, you need to give Google a place to stick its button. You need to add a <div> to the nav-container element that you created in the last chapter. Put it after the <ul> holding the navbar list items, like so:

learnjs/4000/public/index.html

```
<div class='nav-container no-select fixed-top u-full-width'>
  <ul class='inline-list hover-links nav-list six columns'>
    <li><a class='text-lg' href="#">LearnJS</a></li>
    <li><a href="#problem-1">Start</a></li>
  </ul>
  <div class='four columns'>
    <span class='navbar-padding u-pull-right'>
      <span class="g-signin2" data-onsuccess="googleSignIn"></span>
    </span>
  </div>
</div>
```

The g-signin2 class on the <span> tells Google's library to use that element as the container. You'll also need to set the name of the callback function as the data-onsuccess attribute of this element. Because Google's API is going to be inserting a div into this element, you have to style it to get it to lay out properly. Splitting the navbar in half using Skeleton's CSS grid should help. Create two elements: one six columns wide, and the other four columns wide.[6] You'll also need to add a CSS rule with some padding and a display directive, like so:

learnjs/4000/public/index.html

```
.navbar-padding {
  padding-top: 7px;
  display: inline-block;
}
```

---

6. http://getskeleton.com/#grid

With all those parts in place, you should be able to load the app and see a Sign-In button with the Google logo on it appear in the toolbar. Clicking that button opens a new window and redirects you through the connection sequence. You should arrive at the authorization page you configured earlier when you created the Google project in the Developers Console.

Clicking Accept should close the window. In the browser developer console for our application, you should see the callback arguments logged to the console. That means we can now fetch a Google identity in our app. Next, we need to fill in the googleSignIn callback, use the Google ID we received to request the Cognito credentials, and make those credentials available to our app.

Requesting AWS Credentials

Now that we've successfully connected our app with Google through the Sign-In process, we can use the identity token to create a Cognito identity. To do that, we're going to use the AWS SDK for JavaScript to create and configure a CognitoIdentityCredentials object. This object will allow our app to get AWS credentials that it can use to directly access Amazon's web services as an authenticated user. The AWS SDK is already included in the vendor.js file in the prepared workspace.

 If you add other identity providers to this app, you'll need to follow a similar process for each of them.

To create the CognitoIdentityCredentials for a user, we'll need an identity token from Google. You should instantiate this object inside the googleSignIn callback you just wrote. Take a look at this, and we'll walk through it step by step.

learnjs/4103/public/app.js

```
function googleSignIn(googleUser) {
  var id_token = googleUser.getAuthResponse().id_token;
  AWS.config.update({
    region: 'us-east-1',
    credentials: new AWS.CognitoIdentityCredentials({
      IdentityPoolId: learnjs.poolId,
      Logins: {
        'accounts.google.com': id_token
      }
    })
  })
}
```

The first thing you need to do is get the id_token from the response object in googleUser. You need to use this token to create the CognitoIdentityCredentials object. You also need to provide the ID of our identity pool, which you can stash in the namespace object like so:

learnjs/4103/public/app.js

```
var learnjs = {
  poolId: 'us-east-1:aa0e6d15-02da-4304-a819-f316506257e0'
};
```

Once you've created the credentials, you have to update the AWS configuration to include them, along with the Amazon availability region where our identity pool is located. After the configuration has been updated, you need to apply the changes. Then the Cognito user ID will be available to use. The Cognito ID (not the Google one) is what we want to use to identify our users, and it needs to be included on any user record written to the database. However, before we talk about how to get the Cognito ID, we'll need to add a little more behavior to the googleSignIn function to accommodate the life cycle of the Google token we just received.

Refreshing Tokens

The token we get from Google is temporary and will expire after one hour. You can see the expiration time for yourself by looking at the expires_in or expires_at property on the object returned by getAuthResponse in the googleSignIn function. After that token expires, Cognito will no longer be able to use it to refresh our AWS credentials.

Spy Object

To test[a] this behavior, I used a different kind of spy: a spy object. Just like the spy functions we created before, spy objects stand in for real objects and record how the code interacts with them. I can assert that the credentials are created without having the tests actually create real credentials.

By spying on the CognitoIdentityCredentials constructor function, I can return the spy object instead, so that the appOnReady function uses the spy object. Using the andCallFake function in Jasmine, I can delegate to a function that I pass in, which immediately invokes the callback. This turns what is normally an asynchronous operation into a synchronous one, which keeps my tests fast and reliable.

---

a. https://pragprog.com/titles/brapps/source_code

When that happens, we'll need to get an updated token. Different identity providers offer different mechanisms for refreshing this token. In Google's case, we can refresh the token by using the same Google API we loaded to add the Sign-In button. By calling gapi.auth2.getAuthInstance().signIn(), we can update this token, prompting users to reauthorize the app if they've signed out.

To trigger this, create a function named refresh. You can define this function inside the googleSignIn function, because you'll only need it in that scope. You'll be able to use this function (usually in response to a failed request) to update the identity token and refresh the AWS credentials when they expire.

 Details about the Cognito identity are kept in localStorage.[7]

Inside the refresh function, you can invoke signIn and return the object that the Google API returns. Setting the prompt option to login prevents users from having to needlessly reauthenticate if they're already signed in. Attaching a then handler lets you update the AWS credentials object when the request returns successfully.

learnjs/4200/public/app.js

```
function refresh() {
  return gapi.auth2.getAuthInstance().signIn({
      prompt: 'login'
    }).then(function(userUpdate) {
    var creds = AWS.config.credentials;
    var newToken = userUpdate.getAuthResponse().id_token;
```

---

7. https://developer.mozilla.org/en-US/docs/Web/API/Window/localStorage

```
    creds.params.Logins['accounts.google.com'] = newToken;
    return learnjs.awsRefresh();
  });
}
```

Note how the identity token can be updated without re-creating the credentials object. The last step is to update the AWS credentials, which we can encapsulate in a function named learnjs.awsRefresh. As you'll see in the next section, the object returned from that function can be used to chain all of these update requests together in an elegant way.

Identity Requests with Deferred Objects and Promises

When you make changes to the AWS.config.credentials[8] object, you need to call the refresh method on that object when you're done to apply our changes. This function takes a callback that you can use to check if the refresh was successful. The problem is, this refresh process is just one step in a long chain of asynchronous events that you'll have to coordinate whenever the Google token expires. Unless we want our code to be littered with callbacks inside of callbacks, we need a better way to manage this request.

One way to handle this problem would be to use a *Promise*. The Promise/A+ standard specifies a type of object that can be used to coordinate asynchronous events and chain them together. Requests can run asynchronously and then be joined when they are both complete. We can also easily pass the result of one request into the next. Any object that meets the standard can interoperate with other implementations. For example, the call to signIn in the refresh function we just looked at returns an object that meets this standard. The problem with Promises is that not all browsers offer their own implementation yet.

Until we have full support for Promises, we can use jQuery Deferred objects. Similar to Promises, jQuery Deferred objects are a way to perform an action whenever an asynchronous action or request is resolved. Deferred objects can exist in one of three states: *pending*, *resolved*, or *rejected*. When we first create the Deferred, it is in the *pending* state. We can attach callbacks to the Deferred via functions like done, fail, or always. These callbacks will be invoked when the Deferred transitions to the *resolved* (done) or *rejected* (fail) states. When a Deferred is resolved, you can provide a value that will be passed to the callback given to the done method. Unlike an event listener, if the Deferred is already resolved or rejected when you attach the callback, it will be invoked immediately.

---

8.   http://docs.aws.amazon.com/AWSJavaScriptSDK/latest/AWS/Credentials.html

> ⊌/   **Joe asks:**
> ⌇⌇   **But You Promised?!**
>
> Given my preference for web standards, you might be wondering why we're not using a Promise/A+ compatible object to manage our identity information. Since Promises aren't available in all browsers yet, I'm falling back to Deferred objects because I know they'll work, and I'm trying to limit the tools I use in this tutorial.
>
> However, in jQuery 3, Deferred objects *will* be Promise/A+ compatible. So when that's released, even if ECMAScript 6 hasn't made its way into all the browsers yet, we'll be able to use a web standard to manage these chained requests. Unfortunately, at the time of this writing, jQuery 3 is still in Alpha and not suitable for use in this tutorial.

The first place we can use a Deferred is a new function named learnjs.awsRefresh that we'll use to apply the AWS config changes. This function can simply wrap up the callback we pass to the refresh function, resolving it if the request succeeds, and rejecting it if the request fails.

learnjs/4200/public/app.js

```
learnjs.awsRefresh = function() {
  var deferred = new $.Deferred();
  AWS.config.credentials.refresh(function(err) {
    if (err) {
      deferred.reject(err);
    } else {
      deferred.resolve(AWS.config.credentials.identityId);
    }
  });
  return deferred.promise();
}
```

In the last section, we invoked this learnjs.awsRefresh from our refresh function inside googleSignIn. We have to refresh the AWS credentials after updating the Google token ID, and chaining all these requests together with Deferred objects and the Promise objects returned by Google's API makes things a lot easier.

Whenever we use the AWS credentials provided by Cognito, we'll want to keep this refresh function handy. As we'll see in the next chapter, being able to refresh these credentials when an error occurs keeps our users from having to take more drastic measures (like reloading the app) when the token times out. Using the returned Promise, we can easily resubmit the request after refreshing the credentials.

The last thing we'll need to do in the googleSignIn function is apply the AWS configuration we created when we initially received the Google token. Once we do that, we can create an identity object that will hide all these vendor-specific identity management details from the rest of our application.

Creating an Identity Deferred

To manage the identity in our app, we're going to use another Deferred object. This lets a view or any other part of our app take action when users log in, and safely access the profile information to perform those actions. We can create the identity Deferred in the namespace of our application like so:

learnjs/4103/public/app.js

```
learnjs.identity = new $.Deferred();
```

The last step in the googleSignIn function will be to call learnjs.awsRefresh and resolve this Deferred. Any views or other parts of our app that want to perform actions when users log in will be able to do so by attaching a done handler to the Deferred. You can resolve this Deferred with an object that will provide access to the Cognito ID, the refresh function, and other profile information, such as a user's email address.

learnjs/4200/public/app.js

```
learnjs.awsRefresh().then(function(id) {
  learnjs.identity.resolve({
    id: id,
    email: googleUser.getBasicProfile().getEmail(),
    refresh: refresh
  });
});
```

Asynchronous Testing with Jasmine

In the tests for this code, I took advantage of the asynchronous support in Jasmine.[a] By adding an optional done argument to my test function, I was able to make the test wait for the chain of Promises to resolve before making any assertions about the state of the ID token after calling refresh. While this isn't as much of a problem with jQuery 2, it means my tests should keep passing once I upgrade to jQuery 3 and start using Promise/A+ Deferred objects.

Additionally, I completely mocked out the calls to Google's gapi library, because I didn't want to include that library in my tests. Making liberal use of Jasmine's create-SpyObj function makes this pretty straightforward. Check out the example code and tests on pragprog.com if you have questions about how this works.

a. http://jasmine.github.io/2.0/introduction.html#section-Asynchronous_Support

Because this information is available through an identity Promise, we can call it without depending on any specific identity provider. So whether users log in with Google, Facebook, or another service, the rest of our app will never need to know the difference. No matter what identity providers you use, the structure of the object resolved in this Deferred can always be the same.

Now that we've created a Cognito identity for our users, let's do something with it. We're going to create a *profile view* that users can use to see how they're connected to our app. Not only will this be a useful view, but it will give us a way to see our new identity management at work.

Creating a Profile View

An essential aspect of building modern web apps is informing users what information we have about them. A basic way to do this is just to show them all the information we have, so we're going to do that in a new view called the profile view. We'll create this view just like our other views, by adding a route and a view function. Start by adding the view function, like so:

learnjs/4200/public/app.js

```
learnjs.profileView = function() {
  var view = learnjs.template('profile-view');
  learnjs.identity.done(function(identity) {
    view.find('.email').text(identity.email);
  });
  return view;
}
```

Next, you'll need a view template. In this view template, add a simple header and a title.

learnjs/4200/public/index.html

```
<div class='profile-view'>
  <h3>Your Profile</h3>
  <div class='email'></div>
</div>
```

Once that's ready, you can add the route.

learnjs/4200/public/app.js

```
var routes = {
  '#problem': learnjs.problemView,
  '#profile': learnjs.profileView,
  '#': learnjs.landingView,
  '': learnjs.landingView
};
```

To access our new view, you can add a link to the navbar, similar to what you did for the problem view. Instead of adding this link from the view itself, however, you can attach a callback to our identity deferred in the appOnReady. Then, whenever users log in, they'll be able to access the profile view to see what information we're using.

learnjs/4300/public/app.js

```
learnjs.appOnReady = function() {
  window.onhashchange = function() {
    learnjs.showView(window.location.hash);
  };
  learnjs.showView(window.location.hash);
  learnjs.identity.done(learnjs.addProfileLink);
}
```

To add this link when the identity deferred resolves, first create a link template.

learnjs/4301/public/index.html

```
<div class='profile-link navbar-padding-lg'>
  <a href="#profile"></a>
</div>
```

Then you'll need to create an addProfileLink function and add the signin-bar class to the <div> in the navbar that holds the Sign-In button. This will give you a way to prepend the link template when users log in.

learnjs/4300/public/app.js

```
learnjs.addProfileLink = function(profile) {
  var link = learnjs.template('profile-link');
  link.find('a').text(profile.email);
  $('.signin-bar').prepend(link);
}
```

learnjs/4300/public/index.html

```
<div class='four columns signin-bar'>
  <span class='navbar-padding u-pull-right'>
    <span class="g-signin2" data-onsuccess="googleSignIn"></span>
  </span>
</div>
```

Now if you load the application, you should see your email address as a link in the navbar. Clicking this link should show the profile view. Additionally, an *authenticated* identity should now be in the application's identity pool. If you open up the Cognito identity browser page we saw earlier in the AWS console, you should see a new authenticated identity with a linked login.

Identities

Search by Identity ID		Search

| | Results per page | 10 ▾ | ‹ Showing 1 - 2 of 2 › |

Identity ID	Date created (UTC)	Linked logins
us-east-1:8209b940-e6c0-1743-8bf2-9c6a5e40dc3e	2015-06-24T01:25:04Z	1
us-east-1:bfb9c40c-6c13-434a-b22f-a23e659b28b1	2015-05-21T14:09:54Z	0

‹ Showing 1 - 2 of 2 ›

Success! Our app is now connected with a Google ID, which we're using to get authenticated AWS credentials. We have a view that shows some details about the user, and that gives us confidence that our identity management is working. In the next chapter, we'll use these credentials to make web service requests to Amazon Web Services. You'll see how to configure DynamoDB to safely store data specific to one user.

Deploy Again

Now that we have a way for users to connect with our app and view their profile information, it's time to deploy. In particular, it would be good to confirm that the URLs we entered in the project configuration in the Google Developers Console are correct. This isn't something we can verify easily with a unit test or in our development environment. We could try this in a test environment, but that wouldn't really help either unless the URLs were the same. We want to make sure this really works in production before building user visible features on top of it.

So go ahead and deploy the app using the same ./sspa deploy_bucket command we used in *Creating an S3 Bucket*, on page 18. After that's complete, bring up the app in a browser and give it quick tour while we consider what's next.

Next Steps

Now that you've connected the application with Google using Amazon Cognito, you might want to investigate these additional topics. To keep things simple, I didn't cover them in the book, but you might want to explore these topics on your own before moving on to the next chapter.

Connect with Facebook

Setting up Facebook access[9] for our app is similar to setting up access to Google. You go to the Facebook developer portal and create a new App, then get an App ID, similar to Google's Client ID. Facebook provides a Getting Started guide that outlines adding the connect button.

Connect with OpenID

OpenID Connect[10] is a competing standard to OAuth2 that is much more defined, but unfortunately, less popular. However, a few providers offer it, including Salesforce.com and Google. Cognito has a mechanism for connecting to compliant OpenID providers, so it's an option for our app.

Expanding Your Test Environment

Just as with our S3 bucket, if you're creating a test environment, you'll probably want to add an identity pool to it. Simply go through the same steps in this chapter, choosing a different name for your identity pool. You don't need to create another Google application, though.

Developer-Authenticated Identities

You don't have to let Amazon host your identity information to be able to issue temporary AWS credentials with Cognito. Using developer-authenticated identities,[11] you can build your own authentication process and still use Cognito to grant credentials that allow access to AWS resources. If you're integrating with an existing authorization system, you may want to look into this approach.

In the next chapter, we're going to enhance our app to save the answers provided by the users. We'll connect to DynamoDB, add an IAM policy to the Cognito role we just created, and see why data validation is more complex than you might think.

---

9.   http://docs.aws.amazon.com/cognito/latest/developerguide/facebook.html
10. http://docs.aws.amazon.com/cognito/latest/developerguide/open-id.html
11. http://docs.aws.amazon.com/cognito/devguide/identity/developer-authenticated-identities/

CHAPTER 5

Storing Data in DynamoDB

Everything we've built up until now has depended on what we're about to do. We created an application that is hosted entirely in the browser and has no middle tier. We connected this application to Amazon Cognito to create an identity that we can use to access Amazon's other web services directly. Now it's time to connect to those services.

Storing data is something that most web applications do, whether they have a single page or many. In this chapter, you'll see how serverless web apps can interact with Amazon's DynamoDB database service. As we explore this approach, you'll begin to understand the inherent trade-offs. You'll see what steps are necessary to ensure data integrity, and you'll learn how to structure your data to achieve consistent and scalable query performance. By the end of the chapter, you'll know how—and when—to interact directly with a database right from the browser.

Before you start reading and writing data, you need to understand the service you're working with. DynamoDB is a powerful tool, but knowing both its benefits and limitations is crucial to using it effectively. As we'll see in the next section, it all begins with the structure of the data.

Working with DynamoDB

DynamoDB has its roots in the Dynamo key-value store. Amazon created Dynamo in response to a number of critical outages that occurred during the 2004 holiday shopping season.[1] Now the next generation of this system—DynamoDB—is available as a web service that you can use for your own projects.

---

1. http://www.allthingsdistributed.com/2012/01/amazon-dynamodb.html

One of Amazon's goals with DynamoDB was to create a datastore that could scale without limit, and it seems to have achieved that.[2] There are no practical limits on the number of items you can store in a DynamoDB table or how big the table can be. In other words, as long as you keep paying your bill, Amazon will keep adding capacity.

Along with these amazing capabilities, DynamoDB has some quirks. To understand how to organize your data in DynamoDB, you have to pull back the covers and understand a little about how it works. For example, to get the predictable query performance that Amazon claims, you have to understand how DynamoDB handles primary keys and hashing. If you've only worked with relational databases before, some of these things might seem a little counterintuitive.

Understanding DynamoDB Keys and Hashing

DynamoDB organizes data into tables, just like a relational database. But the content of the tables is a little different. Rather than storing records as rows that match a fixed set of columns, DynamoDB lets you store *items* that have an arbitrary set of *attributes*. Each attribute has a name and a value. The only required attributes on an item are the primary key attributes that identify it. This primary key can have either one or two *dimensions*.

Multidimensional Keys

DynamoDB works by mapping multidimensional keys to a value. A multidimensional key is simply a key made up of many parts. For example, a three-dimensional key might consist of a property name, a SHA-1 string, and an integer timestamp. All of these parts combine together to uniquely map to a value.

If the primary key has one dimension, its value must be unique. Amazon calls this one-dimensional key a *hash primary key*. Hash primary keys are stored in an unordered fashion, and their values can be strings, numbers, or binary.

If the primary key has two dimensions, the first is called the *hash attribute*, and the second is called the *range attribute*. In this case, the items in the table are kept sorted by the range attribute. If you've used a composite key in a relational database, this two-dimensional key might sound similar. However, because of the way that DynamoDB is structured, queries that check the range attribute are very efficient and scalable. When querying for

---

2. http://docs.aws.amazon.com/amazondynamodb/latest/developerguide/Limits.html

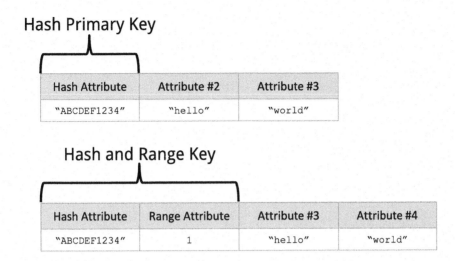

this attribute, you can efficiently apply conditions to ensure the range attribute values are greater or less than a given value, or in between a range of values.

DynamoDB as a Document Database

DynamoDB is fundamentally a key-value store, but it can be used as a document database, so that's how we're going to use it in our app. As long as the objects in our data model meet the constraints that DynamoDB enforces, we'll be able to use it to store JavaScript objects without having to do the work of mapping them back and forth to database rows.

Items in DynamoDB can be up to 400KB in size. This size includes both the names of the attributes and their values, but it wouldn't include any braces or commas that would show up in a JSON representation of an item. The documents in our app should be well under this limit.

In addition to the item size limit, attribute names cannot be longer than 255 bytes. Keep in mind that many Unicode characters are encoded with multiple bytes in UTF-8, so the number of characters isn't necessarily the same as the number of bytes when using UTF-8. Although we'll probably want to avoid using obscure Unicode characters as attribute names in our data model, we'll want to ensure we stay well under the 255 byte limit.

DynamoDB supports a range of types for attribute values. Attributes can be a *scalar type*, such as Number, String, Binary, or Boolean. When sent in a request, binary values should be encoded as Base64 strings. Attributes values can also be NULL, but they cannot be empty (zero bytes).

DynamoDB also supports *multivalued types*, such as String Set, Number Set, and Binary Set. So the value of an attribute can be a collection of other values, like this:

```
{
  firstName: "Robert",
  lastName: "Dole",
  nickNames: ["Bob", "Bobby", "Rob"]
}
```

In addition, you can have attributes with document types, like Lists and Maps.

```
{
  firstName: "Robert",
  lastName: "Dole",
  nickNames: ["Bob", "Bobby", "Rob"],
  addresses: [{
    label: "home",
    street: "123 Fake St.",
    city: "Anytown",
    state: "NY",
    postalCode: "12345"
  }, {
    label: "work",
    street: "456 Phony Ln.",
    city: "Nowheresburg",
    state: "CA",
    postalCode: "54321"
  }]
}
```

DynamoDB tables don't require a schema. The attributes on each item in a table can be different. Unlike a relational database, this means that changes to your document format don't require a schema migration. Depending on the type of change, you may not have to do anything to the existing data. For example, adding an attribute can usually be done entirely in the app. If necessary, you can keep multiple data formats in the database simultaneously, and you can rely on your application to manage the differences.

By using DynamoDB this way, we can write the JavaScript objects in our data model directly to the database. If we query these records back out, the result will be JavaScript objects that we can directly insert into our data model. By adapting our data model to fit the nature of the service, we're able to easily take advantage of the benefits of DynamoDB.

> \\//
> ·ʃ **Joe asks:**
> ## So, Relational Databases Are Bad?
>
> Like most technology decisions, choosing a datastore means choosing between trade-offs. Whether you choose a relational database, a document database, an object database, a key-value store, or just a bunch of files, each option has benefits and disadvantages that you need to consider in the context of your application. Organizing data into tables and rows often makes it easy to analyze. Schemas ensure that data is consistent across records. Moving responsibility for maintaining data integrity out of the database and into the app means you have to be aware of how your data model has changed over time. This can be powerful, but as they say, with great power comes great responsibility.
>
> In this app, I'm using a document database not because I think it's better than a relational database, but because I think it's better than a key-value store. I want to use DynamoDB for the scalability and cost benefits, but out of the box it's essentially a big hash map. The trade-off for using DynamoDB is that we're going to have to do a lot of things that a relational database would normally do for us, but being able to use it to store whole documents instead of individual values makes things a lot easier.

Strong vs. Eventual Consistency

When you write data to DynamoDB and then immediately try to read it, you may not get the same value you just wrote. This behavior is called *eventual consistency*, and it's common in many distributed datastores. It's important to understand why it happens and what you can do to prevent it...although in some cases, you may not want to.

While DynamoDB only has one basic way to write data, it has two ways to read it. You can perform an *eventually consistent* read or a *strongly consistent* read. Which one you choose depends on the situation, and they both have their trade-offs.

Strongly consistent reads are what you normally think of when you read data from a database. This operation returns "the most up-to-date data that reflects updates by all prior related write operations to which DynamoDB returned a successful response."[3] However, these kinds of reads are more likely to fail in the case of a network outage, and perhaps more importantly, they cost more money. As we'll see later in this chapter, you need to purchase more capacity to perform strongly consistent reads.

---

3.   http://docs.aws.amazon.com/amazondynamodb/latest/developerguide/HowItWorks.DataConsistency.html

That means normally we want to design our app to be able to handle eventually consistent reads. The first question you might ask is, how eventual are the reads? DynamoDB's documentation states that "Consistency across all copies of data is usually reached within a second."[4] In practice, this means that you can generally rely on eventually consistent reads for operations that require human interaction. Anything done programmatically should use a strongly consistent read, but we could work around this in the application logic, since anything written to the database in our application would first be available in the data model.

Now that you understand what DynamoDB can and can't do for us, it's time to dive in and create a table. You'll see how to define our primary keys, allocate read/write capacity, and create indexes to improve query performance. You'll also see how we can integrate Cognito identities into our table by defining a security policy that only allows access to authorized users.

Creating a Table

To create this table, you can use the sspa script in the prepared workspace. Just as with the identity pool we created in the last chapter, an action in the script will create and configure all the necessary resources for us. The two AWS CLI commands the script uses to do this are dynamodb create-table and iam put-role-policy. Also, just as before, we're going to walk through what this script is doing for us, so there's no mystery to it.

There's a preconfigured table in the prepared workspace, with a configuration you can use or change to your liking. It's located in conf/dynamodb/tables/learnjs/. Open the config.json file in that directory and take a look.

learnjs/5000/conf/dynamodb/tables/learnjs/config.json

```
{
  "AttributeDefinitions": [
    {
      "AttributeName": "problemId",
      "AttributeType": "N"
    },
    {
      "AttributeName": "userId",
      "AttributeType": "S"
    }
  ],
  "KeySchema": [
    {
```

---

4.   https://aws.amazon.com/dynamodb/faqs/#Read_Consistency

```
      "KeyType": "HASH",
      "AttributeName": "userId"
    },
    {
      "KeyType": "RANGE",
      "AttributeName": "problemId"
    }
  ],
  "ProvisionedThroughput": {
    "ReadCapacityUnits": 5,
    "WriteCapacityUnits": 5
  }
}
```

This file is passed to the dynamodb create-table command, and it specifies the configuration for the table. The three top-level attributes—AttributeDefinitions, KeySchema, and ProvisionedThroughput—are all required parameters for this configuration. Let's look at what these settings mean, and then take a look at some of the optional settings we haven't specified yet.

Attributes and Keys

Attributes in DynamoDB not only have names and values, but they also have types. As you saw earlier, these can be simple types like Strings and Numbers, or they can be more complex types like Maps and Lists. When writing data to a table, the AWS SDK for JavaScript attempts to detect an appropriate type for an attribute, based on the data that's in the object being saved.

However, you may want to define these attribute types up front, if you know what they're going to be. In our case, we know that we're going to need a number problemId attribute, and a string userId attribute. These types are specified with the AttributeType property and a string value that represents the type. The list of available types and their representations is available in the AWS documentation.[5] In this case, we have an "N" for the number type, and an "S" for the string type.

It's worth noting that you don't *need* to specify attribute definitions ahead of time. DynamoDB doesn't require a fixed record schema, and you can add new attributes to any record you write to the database. You have to include the property in the config.json file in order to create the table, but you don't have to add all the attributes you want on your records. The AWK SDK will auto-detect your attribute types when you write records with new attributes.

---

5. http://docs.aws.amazon.com/amazondynamodb/latest/APIReference/API_AttributeValue.html

As you also saw in the last section, DynamoDB has two options for the structure of a table's primary key. In our case, we want to add a *sort* key (also called a range key). By using the Cognito identity ID as the hash key, and the problem number as the range key, we'll be able to not only provide fast query access to the items in this table, but also authorize users to only be able to access the data they create for themselves.

The KeySchema property in config.json lets us define the settings we want for this table's primary keys. Adding two objects to this array—one for the HASH key, and one for the RANGE key—lets us specify which attributes in the record will make up our multidimensional key. Note that the order of the keys matters. The first one must be the HASH key, and the RANGE key, if specified, must be the second one. Although this property is an array, multiple HASH and RANGE keys are not allowed.

Provisioned Throughput

A critical thing to understand about any web service, including DynamoDB, is how you pay for it. Certain costs are associated with data storage and data transfer, but we don't need to be concerned about that when creating a table. All we need to figure out right now is what the *ProvisionedThroughput* setting on our table should be.

With DynamoDB, you purchase the capacity to do read and write operations up front. This capacity is measured in read and write *units*, and you can increase or decrease the capacity on demand to meet the needs of your app. Each read unit gives you the capability to perform one strongly consistent read per second, of an item 4KB or smaller. Using an eventually consistent read gives you two such reads per second for each read capacity unit you allocate. A unit of write capacity allows you to write one item per second, of 1KB or less. These units scale linearly—that is, doing a strongly consistent read, an item of 40KB will use ten read capacity units, and writing five items of 1KB in less than a second will consume five write capacity units.

You can change your provisioned throughput whenever you like to meet the needs of your app. You can provision up to 40,000 read capacity units per table through the AWS console or APIs. Beyond that, you need to contact Amazon support. Amazon's claim is that DynamoDB can scale without limits, but as you can imagine, Amazon wants a little heads up.

When provisioning throughput, you need to consider how random the application's query patterns are. Amazon recommends that you choose primary keys that evenly distribute your query load across the hash space. This is because DynamoDB splits the total key space up into partitions, and it assigns a fraction of your data (and throughput capacity) to each partition.[6] So you might normally think that your provisioned throughput applies to the entire table. However, if your app doesn't query evenly across the keys in the table, you can run into capacity problems while still staying below the total capacity you've allocated.

If the app exceeds the allocated capacity, any request it makes to DynamoDB will result in a ProvisionedThroughputExceededException. Our primary key is a userId, so what this means for our app is that if we have one user who is performing a disproportionate number of read and write operations, it's possible that user may start running into capacity errors when nobody else is seeing a problem. Whether this is a bug or a feature is up to you to decide.

To specify the provisioned throughput for our new table, we need to set the ReadCapacityUnits and WriteCapacityUnits properties in the config object. The example config in the prepared workspaces has these set to five, but the AWS Free Tier provides up to twenty-five read and write capacity units for free across all of your DynamoDB tables. If you're creating two tables for production and test environments, you might want to split this up between the two; otherwise, you can set this as high as twenty-five without adding to your AWS bill.

 You can divide your Free Tier throughput capacity among multiple tables.

Now that you understand what throughput capacity is, go ahead and save any changes you've made to the config.json file. You'll be able to change this as needed, so it's not critical to get it right the first time. However, if you start seeing errors in your application, you'll likely want to change these values right away. You can change them using the AWS CLI tool, or by adjusting the table settings in the AWS web console.

This table has other settings that we're not specifying in config.json. Before moving on, let's take a look at another option you have when creating DynamoDB tables. Although you might not need it now, when it comes time to scale your application up, it may become an essential part of your app.

---

6. http://docs.aws.amazon.com/amazondynamodb/latest/developerguide/GuidelinesForTables.html#Guidelines-ForTables.Partitions

Secondary Indexes and Query vs. Scan

There are two primary methods of getting data out of a DynamoDB table. A *query* efficiently selects items out of the table based on primary key values—hash, or hash and range, depending on the structure of the key. When using a range key, queries can quickly select a subset of the items in the table that meet the conditions of the query.

The other way to get data out of a table is by using a *scan*. A scan evaluates every item in the table, and it can be much slower than a query. By default, a scan returns all the items in the table (up to a limit of 1MB of data), but you can narrow the results by providing a filter expression. However, just like a regular scan, this expression will be evaluated against every item in the table.

Running a scan against a table can be slow if the table contains too much data, even if the results only contain a handful of items. To get around this, you can query against a *secondary index*[7] instead. There are two kinds of secondary indexes: global and local.

A global secondary index contains a copy of the data in a table, but is indexed with different primary keys to allow for fast access. Local secondary indexes use the same hash key as the table, but provide an additional range key, based on one of the attributes on the items in the table. Global secondary indexes can have either a hash or hash and range primary key, and the primary key of a global secondary index can be made up of any attributes in the table.

 Global secondary indexes need their own provisioned throughput.

While it's only possible to create local secondary indexes when you create the table, you can create global secondary indexes later, if you need to. Keep this in mind as your applications grow. We don't need to create any secondary indexes for our application right now, but as the data model evolves and the size of the tables starts to scale up, we may want to add them to maintain acceptable performance characteristics. Creating one or more global secondary indexes can be a quick and easy way to resolve query performance issues.

---

7.   http://docs.aws.amazon.com/amazondynamodb/latest/developerguide/SecondaryIndexes.html

Now that you understand all the options in our table configuration, it's time to run the command to create the table. You'll need to specify both the configuration directory and the name of the identity pool with users who are allowed to access the table, like so:

```
learnjs $ ./sspa create_table conf/dynamodb/tables/learnjs/ learnjs
```

The reason you need to provide the name of the identity pool is that the sspa script also creates the necessary IAM policy to allow access to those users. In the next section, we'll take a look at that generated policy and see how Cognito and DynamoDB can work together to allow safe and secure direct access to the database.

Authorizing DynamoDB Access

Traditional web applications often enforce data access policies with application logic. This typically means performing a database query to fetch user profile information, and then based on that information and the type and content of the request, either rejecting the request or executing it. Any such checks need to run in a secure environment, such as an application server, in order to be effective.

As we'll see in the next chapter, it's possible for serverless applications to perform arbitrary security checks with application logic, but another solution is to control access in a completely data-driven fashion. With our application, for example, we can do that using the *fine-grained access control*[8] facilities provided by DynamoDB.

Before we start enforcing rules for access, let's figure out what we want them to be. We want users to be able to create documents in the learnjs table. This table will contain any correct answers they enter into the app. We also want them to be able to read any document they created, and only update the documents that they own. Users should not be able to access other users' documents (at least, not directly), and they shouldn't have access to any other tables in DynamoDB.

To enforce these rules, the sspa script has created an IAM policy. The script adds an inline policy to the authenticated user role associated with the identity pool you specified when creating the table. You can see an example of the policy here:

---

8. http://docs.aws.amazon.com/amazondynamodb/latest/developerguide/FGAC_DDB.html

learnjs/5001/conf/dynamodb/tables/learnjs/role_policy.json

```
{
  "Version": "2012-10-17",
  "Statement": [{
      "Effect": "Allow",
      "Action": [
        "dynamodb:BatchGetItem",
        "dynamodb:BatchWriteItem",
        "dynamodb:DeleteItem",
        "dynamodb:GetItem",
        "dynamodb:PutItem",
        "dynamodb:Query",
        "dynamodb:UpdateItem"
      ],
      "Resource": ["arn:aws:dynamodb:us-east-1:730171000947:table/learnjs"],
      "Condition": {
        "ForAllValues:StringEquals": {
          "dynamodb:LeadingKeys": ["${cognito-identity.amazonaws.com:sub}"]}
    }
  }]
}
```

In the Action section of this policy, you can see we're granting permission for all relevant DynamoDB operations. The Resource entry restricts these permissions to just our DynamoDB table, which is identified by the ARN. The Condition entry in this policy uses a *substitution variable* to grab the Cognito ID from the request. This ensures that only authenticated Cognito users can access the table, and that they have access only to the documents that they created.

With both the table and the policy created, authenticated Cognito users will be granted access to read and write records to the DynamoDB table. Only the records for that user will be accessible. Now all we have to do is add this behavior to our application.

Saving Documents

Now that we've created our table and authorized our app to connect to it, let's save some data. When the user enters a correct answer, we're going to save it. If they return to this problem later, we'll show them the correct answer they entered before. To add this functionality to the app, you'll first need to change the click handler in the problem view to capture the user input and create an object. Then we'll see how to save that object to DynamoDB.

When writing objects to DynamoDB, we can use the DynamoDB.DocumentClient to interact with DynamoDB like a document database. The objects we store are represented as items with the object properties as attributes, and the values can be either primitive values likes Strings and Numbers, or complex values like Objects and Arrays. The attributes across each item can be different.

One of the great things about the methods on DynamoDB.DocumentClient is that they return a AWS.Request object. This object encapsulates an asynchronous request. You can attach event listeners to the object to be notified when the request succeeds or fails (or when a number of other events occur).

Next, we're going to look at one way to take advantage of this. We'll create a generic function for sending database requests that encapsulates error handling. We'll then use this function to save an item to DynamoDB. While you can interact with the DynamoDB API in many different ways, this approach will give you a good understanding of what DynamoDB is capable of, and will give you insight into common errors that you'll need to be able to handle.

A Fail-Safe Data Access Function

This function, named sendDBRequest, provides access to DynamoDB. A lot is going on here, so we'll walk through it step by step.

learnjs/5200/public/app.js

```
learnjs.sendDbRequest = function(req, retry) {
  var promise = new $.Deferred();
  req.on('error', function(error) {
    if (error.code === "CredentialsError") {
      learnjs.identity.then(function(identity) {
        return identity.refresh().then(function() {
          return retry();
        }, function() {
          promise.reject(resp);
        });
      });
    } else {
      promise.reject(error);
    }
  });
  req.on('success', function(resp) {
    promise.resolve(resp.data);
  });
  req.send();
  return promise;
}
```

First, we create a new Deferred object. Creating this object and returning it from the sendDbRequest function allows you to chain this with other asynchronous requests. Once you've created the Deferred, you can attach two event handlers to the request via the on method—one for the error and one for success.

A successful response is easy enough to handle. As you can see on line 17, we resolve the Deferred object with the data in the response. Handling the error event is a little more involved. As you saw in the last chapter, AWS credentials expire after one hour, and you have to refresh them. If our request to DynamoDB fails with a CredentialsError,[9] then we know the credentials need to be refreshed. In the last chapter, we added a function to the identity object to refresh the credentials. Checking for this error code on an errored response object lets us know this is the place to use it, as we do on line 4.

The call to identity.refresh in the error callback refreshes the identity provider token and AWS credentials. Because identity.refresh returns a promise, once the credentials have been refreshed we can resubmit the request via a callback passed to the then method, by invoking the retry callback on line 7.

If the DynamoDB request fails for any other reason, we simply reject the Deferred on line 13. Rejecting or resolving the promise with the AWS response will let the caller take specific action if necessary. Once both event handlers are registered, the last step is to actually send the request, which you do with the send method. Callers of sendDbRequest will be able to use the returned promise to react if the request succeeds or fails.

Creating and Saving an Item

Now that we have this generic function to rely on, we can build another function to create DynamoDB items and save them. We'll call this function saveAnswer, and it looks like this:

learnjs/5200/public/app.js

```javascript
learnjs.saveAnswer = function(problemId, answer) {
  return learnjs.identity.then(function(identity) {
    var db = new AWS.DynamoDB.DocumentClient();
    var item = {
      TableName: 'learnjs',
      Item: {
        userId: identity.id,
        problemId: problemId,
        answer: answer
      }
    };
    return learnjs.sendDbRequest(db.put(item), function() {
      return learnjs.saveAnswer(problemId, answer);
    })
  });
};
```

---

9. http://docs.aws.amazon.com/amazondynamodb/latest/developerguide/ErrorHandling.html#APIError

The saveAnswer function creates the item object, adding necessary fields like the Cognito ID. So the first thing we do here is wait for the identity Deferred to resolve. We need to set the userId on the item to be the current user's Cognito ID. If the value is not the same as the ID of the user who's been authenticated with Cognito, this request will fail.

Using Request Callbacks

Instead of attaching event handlers to the Request object returned from DocumentClient.put, you can also pass a callback as a second parameter. This would have made it harder to create the sendDbRequest function, so I chose to use the request object instead. However, you can use this API in many different ways, and the examples in this chapter are meant to inspire and explain, not represent a "best practice."

Once the item has been created, we can invoke DocumentClient.put to create a Request and pass that to sendDbRequest. Remember that sendDbRequest takes a callback that will retry the request in case of a credentials error. Our retry logic is fairly simplistic right now; we simply re-invoke the current function with the current arguments to try again.

 Refactor: pull the declaration for answer out into the surrounding function.

The last step is to use this new function in the checkAnswerClick handler. You'll need to pull the variable declaration for answer up into the surrounding function to be able to access it. You then need to pass the problem number to saveAnswer, along with the value of the answer input element, like so:

learnjs/5200/public/app.js

```
function checkAnswerClick() {
  if (checkAnswer()) {
    var flashContent = learnjs.buildCorrectFlash(problemNumber);
    learnjs.flashElement(resultFlash, flashContent);
    learnjs.saveAnswer(problemNumber, answer.val());
  } else {
    learnjs.flashElement(resultFlash, 'Incorrect!');
  }
  return false;
}
```

Separating the behavior in the saveAnswer and sendDbRequest functions not only gives us a chance to reuse sendDbRequest, but it also makes the code a little easier to read. It also creates a testing boundary that makes it easier to test. Now that we're saving data, the next step is to start fetching it.

Fetching Documents

Now that we put a document in DynamoDB, let's get it back out again. We can reuse sendDbRequest to create a function that fetches a saved answer asynchronously. It should look something like this:

learnjs/5400/public/app.js

```
learnjs.fetchAnswer = function(problemId) {
  return learnjs.identity.then(function(identity) {
    var db = new AWS.DynamoDB.DocumentClient();
    var item = {
      TableName: 'learnjs',
      Key: {
        userId: identity.id,
        problemId: problemId
      }
    };
    return learnjs.sendDbRequest(db.get(item), function() {
      return learnjs.fetchAnswer(problemId);
    })
  });
};
```

Just as with saveAnswer, we need to start by fetching the Cognito ID. Once we have it, we can create the request object, which has a similar structure to the item we just saved. The main difference is that rather than specifying the item to be saved, we create an object that represents the key of the item to be fetched.

Once we've created that object, we can call get to create the AWS Request object and pass that to sendDbRequest. Just as before, we need to supply a retry function in case the credentials have timed out.

With that function in place, we can now attempt to fetch a stored answer for the current problem. Inside the problemView function, we need to make a call to fetchAnswer and attach a handler to the resulting Deferred. When it resolves, we'll have our answer, which we can put in the answer text area in the view.

learnjs/5300/public/app.js

```
learnjs.fetchAnswer(problemNumber).then(function(data) {
  if (data.Item) {
    answer.val(data.Item.answer);
  }
});
```

Now, when a user gets the right answer for a problem, the answer is saved. If the user returns to that problem later or reloads the application, their correct answer will be restored. Users who don't want to log in to save their answers will be able to use the app as before. And if at any point a logged-in user's AWS credentials expire, we'll refresh them and continue on.

We've taken a big step here, but we need to cover one more thing before deploying this change. While it's not a problem for this example, it's important to understand what options you have when validating data written to DynamoDB. As we'll see, the traditional approach won't work in a serverless application, so we're going to have to address this concern differently.

Data Access and Validation

In a traditional web application, the application server typically performs validation of users' requests. For example, before writing a record to the database, the application server might inspect the record for problems related to many different concerns, ranging from user experience to security and data integrity.

In a serverless web application, you have to separate these concerns. Validation done for security reasons cannot be performed in a web client. Anything that our app can do, a user can also do, because browser environments are completely within the control of the user. For example, changing the code in our application is easy to do from the development console in most web browsers, and a malicious user could do this to write data to DynamoDB. Even taking the browser out of the equation, if someone can take the credentials they get from Cognito and issue requests via HTTP, the only thing stopping them from writing to our table is the security policies we have in place.

A web client *can* validate data for user experience reasons, such as ensuring that the user enters a phone number or ZIP code properly. In our case, our app validates that the answer is correct before saving it. But in all cases, this validation is done for the benefit of the user, not for the benefit of the system. Outside of the constraints that can be enforced by the web service, you can make no assumptions about the data in a table that is writable directly from the client.

Although we can perform UX validation in the app, we must perform any data access checks in a web service. DynamoDB provides some facilities for validating requests like this. By expanding the conditions clause in our IAM policy, we can check the properties of the request.

Defining "Valid" Data

There is validation you perform to ensure a good user experience, and there is validation you perform for security reasons. Conflating the two can be dangerous. You can
easily fall into the trap of thinking your data is "safe" because you validated it for
consistency or UX reasons. Ensuring that a user's name is less than 255 characters
doesn't prevent the value from being a SQL injection attack. Thinking of these concerns
as separate things helps ensure they're both addressed effectively.

For example, in our application, we could grant authorized users permission
to perform a count of answers from other users. Our application could then
make a scan request with filter criteria to determine how many users have
answered a particular question, or figure out what the most commonly
answered question is. To do this, we need to create a new policy that grants
this access, and add it to the authenticated Cognito user role using either
the IAM web console or the AWS command-line interface. The policy looks
like this:

```
learnjs/5500/policy/table_policy_condition.json
{
  "Version": "2012-10-17",
  "Statement": [{
      "Effect": "Allow",
      "Action": ["dynamodb:Scan"],
      "Resource": ["arn:aws:dynamodb:us-east-1:730171000947:table/learnjs"],
      "Condition": {
        "ForAllValues:StringEquals": {
          "dynamodb:Select": ["COUNT"]
        }
      }
    }
  }]
}
```

The ForAllValues::StringEquals means DynamoDB ensures each key, such as
dyamodb:Select, matches the specific value in the request. Since we're using
ForAllValues and not ForAnyValue, these checks are joined with a logical *and*, and
any additional keys we add here would also have to match. We can use a
number of different policy keys for these clauses. Some are specific to
DynamoDB requests,[10] and some can be used on any request.[11] For example,
we can limit users to certain attributes in a table with the dynamodb:Attributes

---

10. http://docs.aws.amazon.com/amazondynamodb/latest/developerguide/UsingIAMWithDDB.html#IAMPolicyKeys
11. http://docs.aws.amazon.com/IAM/latest/UserGuide/reference_policies_elements.html#Condition

key, or we can limit access to a specific range of IP addresses with the aws:SourceIp key.

Adding this policy to the authenticated Cognito user role in IAM allows us to send a scan request from the app that would count the answer documents that match any given filter criteria. As you can see in the following code, we can send this request using the same sendDbRequest function that our other DB access functions use. Note the use of the FilterExpression and ExpressionAttribute-Values entries to limit the scope of the results to a particular problem ID.

learnjs/5500/public/app.js

```
learnjs.countAnswers = function(problemId) {
  return learnjs.identity.then(function(identity) {
    var db = new AWS.DynamoDB.DocumentClient();
    var params = {
      TableName: 'learnjs',
      Select: 'COUNT',
      FilterExpression: 'problemId = :problemId',
      ExpressionAttributeValues: {':problemId': problemId}
    };
    return learnjs.sendDbRequest(db.scan(params), function() {
      return learnjs.countAnswers(problemId);
    })
  });
}
```

This request then yields a response object with the Count property, specifying the number of answer documents that have a problemId attribute equal to the number that we passed into the countAnswers function. Without this policy in place, attempting to send this request would result in a error, like this:

```
User: «Role ARN» is not authorized to perform:
  dynamodb:Scan on resource: «Table ARN»
```

As useful as this facility is, some security concerns can't be addressed using the Condition clause. For example, it's currently not possible to validate the data itself using a policy. We can only enforce rules about the type of request, where it's from, who made it, and things like that. So while it's really easy to control access this way, certain situations will require more sophisticated validation than what an IAM policy can provide.

In those cases, you can create a custom web service to handle the request. This web service can inspect the data before writing, or perform arbitrary filtering on query results. Doing this with Amazon's Lambda service is easy, and that's what we're going to do in the next chapter. Before we get to that, however, we should deploy the new functionality we've created.

Deploy Again

In this chapter, we saw how to create and configure a DynamoDB table. You created some functions in our app that can write and read data from this table and gracefully handle credential timeouts. So let's go ahead and deploy our app using the same ./sspa deploy_bucket command we used in Chapter 1. After that's complete, we can bring up our app in a browser and test it out, while we consider what's next.

Next Steps

Now that you understand how DynamoDB works, you might want to investigate these additional topics.

jQuery 3 and Promise/A+ Deferred

We could easily change some of the functions we looked at in this chapter to use A+ Promises, available in either jQuery 3 or ES6. Depending on which one you choose, you might need to change some of the function names. However, the overall effect would be the same. Wrapping up the AWS DocumentClient API in a Promise is a great way to chain asynchronous events together easily and make it easier to integrate DynamoDB with the rest of the application.

Policy Simulator

So all this profile configuration wizardry is cool and all, but it doesn't do you any good unless you can test it. Ensuring that someone *doesn't* have access to something can be tricky. Thankfully, using the IAM Policy Simulator,[12] you can easily check if you've created an access profile correctly. Note that you'll have to sign in to the AWS console to use this tool.

Allowing S3 Access

It doesn't always make sense to put data in a database. Things like images, sounds, and video are best stored in services specifically designed for large media objects. You can use S3 for this, and you can control access to S3 objects using the same techniques we used for DynamoDB. See the AWS documentation[13] for details.

---

12. https://policysim.aws.amazon.com/home/index.jsp
13. http://docs.aws.amazon.com/IAM/latest/UserGuide/access_policies_examples.html#iam-policy-example-s3

CHAPTER 6

Building (Micro)Services with Lambda

While running every line of code needed for your application in the browser may be preferable, it's not always possible. In some situations, creating a custom web service to support your application makes a lot of sense. As we saw in the last chapter, you may want to enforce data constraints that can't be specified in an access policy. You also might want to filter query results before sending them back to the browser, perhaps to save bandwidth costs or to improve user experience on devices with limited or intermittent network access. Providing an additional HTTP interface to your data can also enable third-party access to your app or create opportunities for caching data via browser-supported HTTP caching policies.

Just because we want web services doesn't mean we want web servers. Using Amazon's Lambda service, we can create web services that run in dedicated containers that only cost money when they're actually handling requests. Unlike the Elastic Compute Cloud (EC2) and other virtualized server environments, building a custom web service using Lambda provides the same sort of cost, scalability, and availability benefits that we expect from services like DynamoDB. As we'll see in this chapter, Lambda services are easy to build and maintain, and you can use them to do amazing things with other parts of the AWS ecosystem.

For example, in our app, we can create a Lambda service that will provide the most common answer provided by our users to one of the programming puzzles. We'll be able to do this in a secure way, without compromising access to other user data, and doing it as a custom service will have the additional benefit of reducing the amount of data sent to the browser.

To build our new service, we'll first take a look at the basics of the Lambda environment and how it works. Then we'll define a service using the AWS command-line interface, write the code for our service, and deploy it. We'll finish the chapter by looking at two different methods for invoking our new service. One is an authenticated method using Cognito credentials, and the other is a public method using HTTP.

Understanding Amazon Lambda

Amazon Lambda is a service that lets you run code in the cloud without provisioning or managing servers. With Lambda, Amazon has jumped firmly onto the microservices bandwagon. They might even be pulling the wagon. Lambda lets you write stand-alone functions in JavaScript—and, increasingly, in other languages—that run in a specialized container. You can access these functions in many ways, including over the web via the Amazon API Gateway.

To use Lambda with JavaScript, we need to create a JavaScript function that takes two arguments and put it in a .js file. This function can use anything in the Node.js standard library, or any other Node.js libraries we wish to include. We then need to package this function, and all of its dependencies, in a zip file. Finally, we need to choose a name and any applicable settings like resource limits, and upload the zip file that contains our function to AWS. Then our new service will be ready to use, via whatever methods we've configured it to accept.

To build a new service for our application, let's first understand the runtime environment we're working with when we use Lambda. After that, we'll take a look at Lambda's pricing. As with all Amazon Web Services, the cost of the service informs the decisions we make when designing applications, and that's true for Lambda as well. After you understand the costs, then we'll see how to deploy and build a new Lambda service (in that order).

The Lambda Environment

For this application, we're going to use Node.js to write our Lambda service. Node.js is a JavaScript runtime based on V8, the JavaScript engine found in Google's Chrome web browser. Similar to Ruby's EventMachine and Python's Twisted frameworks, Node.js uses an event-driven model to prevent blocking on I/O and other long-running operations. Unlike these frameworks, the Node.js standard library and open source package community are focused entirely on this event-driven approach, so any operation you perform can be done in a non-blocking fashion.

In addition to Node.js, we have other options for writing Lambda services. Amazon also supports Java and Python Lambda functions, so if you're familiar with those languages, you could just as easily use one of those environments as well. Since this book is about building web apps, we're going to use Node.js, because anyone doing web development should be comfortable using JavaScript.

Why Node.js?

Node.js has gained in popularity in the last few years, but it is not without controversy. Critics decry the sometimes unintuitive nature of asynchronous programming, and question why anyone would build a new runtime on top of JavaScript—a language that, for historical reasons, is filled with idiosyncrasies. Proponents point to the package repository for NPM (the Node.js package manager), which the Node.js foundation claims is the "largest ecosystem of open source libraries in the world,"[a] and praise JavaScript as an easily accessible language with broad appeal and plenty of resources for learning.

You certainly don't need to write Lambda services in JavaScript, as Amazon provides alternatives in the form of Python and Java. Truth be told, on the merits of the language alone, JavaScript would be my last choice out of the three. But JavaScript is a language that demands to be recognized, and we're already using it in our web app.

a.   https://nodejs.org/en/

Regardless of the language you use, all Lambda services run on servers using Amazon's Linux distribution, currently using the 3.14 kernel. You can refer to the AWS documentation[1] to find out the specific version of Linux, if you wish. Accessing the underlying Linux environment from your Lambda service is not only permitted but encouraged, as a way to expand the capabilities of Lambda by running native code.

Lambda services are backed by a single function. The signature for a Lambda function takes two arguments. The first argument is the request payload (similar to the body of an HTTP post), which is expected to be sent as JSON, and delivered to the function as a parsed JavaScript object. The second argument is called the *context*, and it is used to interact with the Lambda environment, including methods to either respond to the request or fail with an error. Here's an example of a simple Lambda function, which you can find in the prepared workspace:

learnjs/1000/services/lib/index.js

```
exports.echo = function(json, context) {
  context.succeed(["Hello from the cloud! You sent " + JSON.stringify(json)]);
};
```

---

1.   http://docs.aws.amazon.com/lambda/latest/dg/current-supported-versions.html

This function immediately calls the succeed method to complete the request and return the argument as the result. Results from Lambda functions are always JSON. JavaScript Lambda functions can yield a JSON-compatible JavaScript object—no need to call JSON.stringify()—so we're using an array to contain our message.

 Lambda functions written in Java pay the JVM startup time penalty when they are invoked infrequently.

It's important to note that Lambda functions don't necessarily exit when the function returns. Until you use the context to either respond to the request or fail, your function may continue to consume compute time. This is an important feature, because if you have asynchronous tasks running, they may not be complete by the time the function returns. Being able to invoke a callback to finish the request makes sense when you're working in the asynchronous environment that Node.js provides. We'll take a closer look at how this works when we create a Lambda function later in this chapter.

If you don't complete the request, but you don't have any pending callbacks, your function will exit with the message "Process exited before completing request." Even if you don't need to return a response from your function, this is a situation you want to avoid, because you're likely paying for more compute time than you need and generating needless errors in your logs.

Lambda Limits

As you may expect, you can't do certain things from a Lambda function. However, there are a surprising number of things you *can* do...things that you may not expect from an environment like Lambda.

For example, you can write to the filesystem of the underlying OS. Each Lambda function gets 512MB of ephemeral disk space on the filesystem, located at /tmp, which you can use for scratch space. However, this space is strictly for use while your function is running. It is not persisted or shared between different execution environments.

You can also shell out and run Linux commands from your function. This allows you to use Node.js libraries with native extensions, or use standard Linux command-line tools to process data. You can even upload your own statically linked Linux binaries and invoke those from your function. The Lambda security model makes no distinctions between what your function is allowed to do and what any subprocesses that you spawn can do.

As with most Linux environments, there are some limits[2] to the number of processes you can spawn and the number of file descriptors you can have open. It also limits the number of concurrent invocations of your function that can be active at one time. By default, this is set to 100, but you can contact Amazon to increase it. Lastly, no matter what settings you've defined for the function, a single execution cannot take more than 300 seconds. Limits like these are in place to prevent a programming error from turning into an expensive computing mistake. To understand exactly how expensive these mistakes might be, let's take a look at how we pay for the services we get with Lambda.

Memory, Time, and Cost

Just as with DynamoDB, Amazon Lambda provides almost unlimited scalability and low-cost high availability. Using it to build our web service means that our application can get extremely popular before we have to start worrying about re-architecting for scale. But in order to use these services effectively, you have to understand how you pay for them. Otherwise, your low-cost solutions can quickly turn into unexpected billing disasters.

You pay to use Lambda by the *gigabyte-second* (or GBS, for short). The longer your function runs and the more memory it uses, the more you have to pay. For example, let's say your function uses 128MB of memory and takes 100ms to run. If it's invoked 100,000 times, then you'll pay for 125GBS, which costs about $0.02 given the currently available pricing.

So the two costs we want to be aware of when writing a Lambda function are the two costs we should probably be thinking about for any program: space (memory) and time. This includes any memory used when shelling out to other processes in the environment, whether they're included in the Amazon Linux distribution or uploaded as part of the function bundle.

The duration of your Lambda function is calculated from the time it begins running to the time it exits. It's not based on how many CPU cycles are used. Making asynchronous requests in parallel, rather than serially, not only ensures that your function performs well, but also keeps your costs low. Additionally, taking advantage of the ephemeral disk space available to Lambda functions is a great way to save memory (potentially at the cost of time, however). Accumulating results on disk might make more sense than keeping them in memory.

---

2. https://docs.aws.amazon.com/lambda/latest/dg/limits.html

Now that we've covered what Lambda can do, what it can't do, and how much it costs, it's time to build something. Just as with our web app, we'll create a new service by deploying something first. Then we'll build a new service specifically for our application.

Deploy First

For all same the reasons we deployed our web app before building it, we're going to deploy a Lambda service before we build one. Along the way, you'll see how you can configure, deploy, and test these services. Rather than starting with a new service, however, we're going to deploy the service we already have. Once we've completed that step successfully, we'll be ready to build a new service and deploy it with confidence.

The service that we're going to deploy is based on the echo function we saw earlier in the chapter. The services directory in the prepared workspace holds all the code for our application's Lambda services, and the echo function code currently lives in this directory as well. In addition to the code, the prepared workspace includes files that control how the individual microservices are configured. Just as with the other services in our app, these configuration files live in the conf directory. Combining these two artifacts together gives us everything we need to deploy a custom web service.

Just as with other tasks, you can use the sspa script to run the AWS CLI commands necessary to deploy this Lambda function. As always, we'll walk through all the steps involved so that you understand what's going on. To deploy this service, first review the example Lambda configuration included in the prepared workspace. Then we'll see how to deploy the echo service and test that it is configured properly.

Configuring a Lambda Function

To get started, open the config.json file in the conf/lambda/functions/echo directory.

learnjs/1000/conf/lambda/functions/echo/config.json

```json
{
    "Runtime": "nodejs",
    "Timeout": 5,
    "MemorySize": 128,
    "Publish": true
}
```

This configuration file is passed to AWS CLI's lambda create-function command.[3] The Runtime property here specifies the runtime environment that the function uses. Options include nodejs, java8 and python2.7. For our services, we're using Node.js, so we need to set this to nodejs.

As we saw earlier, we pay for Lambda functions based on how much memory they use and how long they run. The Timeout and MemorySize properties limit how much memory and time the function can use. The echo function is configured to use no more than 128MB of memory and run for no longer than five seconds. Considering what it's doing, that should be plenty. For our new function, we can start with a reasonable setting and increase it if we start to see problems.

The Publish setting controls whether or not to create an immutable version number when we release a new version of our function. You can reference Lambda functions using these version numbers to ensure the behavior doesn't change unexpectedly. Although we're not using Lambda function versions right now, we'll set this to true in the new service configuration just in case we change our minds later.

Lambda Load Times

For simplicity's sake, all of the function handlers in this app are in one file, index.js. However, as your application grows, you may want to move each function handler out into its own file. Keeping the dependencies for each service separate means that fewer modules need to be loaded when the service starts up, which can improve service response times. We don't have a lot of dependencies for our application's services, so we're not going to do that yet.

In addition to the properties in the config.json file, the sspa script automatically sets the other properties that the lambda create-function command requires. For example, the FunctionName property is set to the name of the configuration directory. The Role property is the ARN of the IAM role this function should assume. The sspa script generates this role using the iam create-role command in the AWS CLI. You can see the configuration for this role here:

---

3. http://docs.aws.amazon.com/cli/latest/reference/lambda/create-function.html

learnjs/6000/conf/iam/roles/learnjs_lambda_exec/info.json

```json
{
    "Role": {
        "AssumeRolePolicyDocument": {
            "Version": "2012-10-17",
            "Statement": [
                {
                    "Action": "sts:AssumeRole",
                    "Principal": {
                        "Service": "lambda.amazonaws.com"
                    },
                    "Effect": "Allow",
                    "Sid": ""
                }
            ]
        },
        "RoleId": "AROAJ67KFEW5PCLEK3X2S",
        "CreateDate": "2015-12-17T18:27:47.499Z",
        "RoleName": "learnjs_lambda_exec",
        "Path": "/",
        "Arn": "arn:aws:iam::730171000947:role/learnjs_lambda_exec"
    }
}
```

In the previous chapter, we used an IAM role to grant permissions to our users. This role isn't as complicated as that one, because the only qualification for assuming it is being a Lambda service. As it is right now, this role has no profiles, and therefore it grants no special access. We'll need to add some profiles to this role to support our new service, but for the echo function, no additional permissions are required.

The Handler property specifies the *function handler*. The function handler is the name of the actual JavaScript function that will be called when the Lambda function is invoked. You specify it by combining the Node.js module (file) and the exported function name. The sspa script assumes that the function name is the same as the configuration directory name, and that all our Lambda functions reside in the index.js file inside the services/lib directory. For example, the handler for the echo function would be index.echo.

Creating the Code Bundle

We need to pack up the code for our Lambda service into a zip file that contains both the functions and their dependencies. This zip file is called a *code bundle.* You will need to build this code bundle in order to upload the configuration for the echo function.

Code bundles can be no larger than 50MB.

To build the code bundle for our services, you'll need to have Node.js installed. Amazon's environment for Lambda currently uses Node.js v4.3.2, and you'll want to use the same version to both run and test your Lambda functions. You'll also need the *NPM* package manager to install dependencies. If you need help installing these tools, you can refer to Appendix 1, *Installing Node.js*, on page 177.

Once you have Node.js and NPM installed, you can test your setup by trying to build the services code bundle. The sspa script creates this bundle as a zip file named archive.zip in the services directory. To build the bundle, you can use the build_bundle action in the script, like so:

```
learnjs $ ./sspa build_bundle
```

If that works, then you should be ready to upload the echo function to AWS. To do that, run the create_service action in the sspa script, like so:

```
learnjs $ ./sspa create_service conf/lambda/functions/echo
```

If that command runs without error, then the echo service should be ready to use. We should probably try it out, right? Of course, we don't have any accessible endpoints for this service, and we don't really want to spend the time to make one, but there is still a way to test it. To do that, return to the AWS web console and open up the controls for the Lambda service.

Testing Functions Through the AWS Console

To test the actual logic of our functions, we're going to write unit tests with Jasmine, just as we did for the application code that runs in the browser. We'll need a different way to test the service configuration we just created. One way is to use the testing facilities built into the AWS console.

If you look at the settings page for your Lambda function, you should see a button in the upper-left corner labeled Test. It looks like this:

If you click this button, you'll be presented with a form that lets you type the body of a request. Request data sent to Lambda functions are always JSON, so whatever you enter here has to be valid JSON. However, since our function is simply going to echo back whatever you send it, the format of the JSON message doesn't matter.

Once you've entered a value, hit Save and Test, and the function will be invoked. The AWS console shows the result at the bottom of the screen, and it also indicates whether the function returned successfully or raised an error. If everything is working correctly, you should see something like this:

```
[
    "Hello from the cloud! You sent {\"problemNumber\":42}"
]
```

If you see a result like this, then you know you've deployed the echo function correctly. Obviously, this is just a *smoke test*. That is, running this test tells us that the function can run, but it doesn't tell us whether it actually works in all cases. This function is simple, but as we create more complex functions, we're going to need a way to test them more completely.

Creating a New Lambda Configuration

Now that we've deployed the configuration for the echo Lambda service, let's create a new configuration for our new service. Then we can write the service and upload the code. To create a configuration for our new function, simply make a copy of the echo directory with the name popularAnswers. Be sure to delete the info.json file in the popularAnswers directory after copying so that the sspa script knows to make a new service. You can then change the config.json file in that new directory as needed.

The echo service configuration is actually quite close to what we'll need for our new service. One thing we'll probably want to do is bump up the maximum memory size from 128MB to 512MB. You can do that by changing the MemorySize property, like so:

learnjs/6001/conf/lambda/functions/popularAnswers/config.json

```
{
    "Runtime": "nodejs",
    "Timeout": 5,
    "MemorySize": 512,
    "Publish": true
}
```

Once you've finished making that change, you can run the sspa script to upload this new configuration to AWS:

```
learnjs $ ./sspa create_service conf/lambda/functions/popularAnswers
```

If that runs without error, then our new service should be configured. It doesn't have any code behind it yet, so there's no point in trying to test it, but we'll remedy that in the next section.

Creating a Test Environment

Although I don't show it here, you'll probably want to create two functions, not just one. Just as with the rest of our app, creating a test environment for this Lambda function will let you verify changes before they're deployed to users, and it will give you a safe development sandbox to work in.

Adding Policies to the Lambda Execution Role

Now that we've created our new service, we need to add some policies to the IAM role that our Lambda services will assume when they run. This role, named learnjs_lambda_exec by the sspa script, needs a policy that allows our Lambda services to access DynamoDB. While you might want to configure these roles individually for each service, we're going to keep things simple by using one role for all the services in our app. This means that all of our services will have the same level of access.

Rather than creating custom policies for our Lambda service role, we're going to use Amazon's *managed policies*. These are canned policies—created and managed by Amazon—which provide access to all the resources in either a specific service or a range of services. To see the list of available managed policies, you can run the iam list-policies command as the admin profile, like so:

```
$ aws --profile admin iam list-policies
{
    "Policies": [
        {
            "PolicyName": "AWSDirectConnectReadOnlyAccess",
            "CreateDate": "2015-02-06T18:40:08Z",
            "AttachmentCount": 0,
            "IsAttachable": true,
            "PolicyId": "ANPAI23HZ27SI6FQMGNQ2",
            "DefaultVersionId": "v1",
            "Path": "/",
            ...
```

The policy we want to add to our Lambda service is named AmazonDynamoDBFullAccess. We'll need the ARN of this policy to add it to the Lambda execution role. ARNs of managed policies are just based on the name. This one is arn:aws:iam::aws:policy/AmazonDynamoDBFullAccess.

To add this policy to our Lambda execution role, we need to call the iam attach-role-policy command in the AWS CLI. We could use the sspa command to do this, but unlike some of the other tasks we've performed in this chapter, using the AWS CLI is just as easy. All we need is the role name and the ARN of the policy, like so:

```
$ aws --profile admin iam attach-role-policy \
  --role-name learnjs_lambda_exec \
  --policy-arn arn:aws:iam::aws:policy/AmazonDynamoDBFullAccess
```

Once this command runs—assuming you don't get any errors—all our Lambda services should have full access to DynamoDB. Since we haven't added an implementation for the new service yet, you can double-check this either by using the iam list-attached-role-policies command in the AWS CLI or by looking at the role in the AWS web console. You should see an attached managed policy, like this:

Now that we've configured a new Lambda service, we're ready to write the actual JavaScript function that will support it. Our new function will need to take a problem number from the request and then fetch all the answers to that problem from the database. It will then need to sort those answers using a comparator and find the most popular ones. Those answers will then be returned as the response.

Writing Lambda Functions

To write the function for our new service, we're simply going to add another function definition to the index.js file. Name this function popularAnswers. Once you deploy this function, you'll be able to use the new service we've created.

Any additional Lambda functions you want to add to this app should be added to this file as well. As those functions grow, you can break out the logic into other modules in the project, included through the standard Node.js module system.[4]

You might wonder why we aren't creating a new project to host this function. After all, one of the supposed benefits of microservices is that they're decoupled from each other. Won't building all of our Lambda functions into a single project create exactly the kind of monolithic mess that microservices are supposed to prevent?

Avoiding Microservice Architecture Problems

Most applications, whether they're web applications or not, are focused on a particular problem domain. Being able to break down that problem domain into ever smaller and simpler solutions is a large part of what makes for a good programmer. Whenever possible, it makes sense to do this.

However, not every problem can be neatly decomposed into discrete components. Even when that's possible, a common challenge when building applications is managing all the interactions between components. Only rarely do we discover a solution that is so general and so decoupled that it warrants extraction into a stand-alone form.

So to understand why you might want to put all of your Lambda functions into a single project, consider what will happen if you don't. If being able to completely decouple the parts of your application is a difficult and rare feat, then beginning with a decoupled architecture would be an act of supreme hubris. It's more likely that you'll have to refactor your design many times before a decoupled, fully encapsulated, reusable, stand-alone service emerges.

If you optimize prematurely by breaking things apart at the outset, and then later discover that you need to refactor *across* services in order to improve

---

4.   https://nodejs.org/api/modules.html#modules_modules

the design, you're going to have a lot more work to do. What would have been one change in a single system might become three. Two commits to a repository might turn into a half dozen spread across a handful of repos. It's quite likely that beginning with separated services will make it less likely that you'll ever wind up with truly decoupled services, because you're just making it harder to improve the design through refactoring.

Creating a single project for our application services allows us to easily share code across services, reuse test data and helper functions to verify interactions between services, and eliminate duplication in our domain model by maintaining a single source of truth. At some point in the future, if it makes sense to extract one or more stand-alone services, then keeping our code in an easily refactored state will make that transition easier.

If poorly designed monolithic systems are a big ball of mud, you could say that poorly designed microservice systems are a swarm of fire ants. You don't want to find either in your backyard on a Sunday afternoon. By deploying all our services from the same bundle, and by using the configuration of each Lambda function to control what code is run, we get to use an awesome service container with the confidence that our services work together.

Microservices and Service-Oriented Architecture

In the late nineties, we had this shiny new thing called service-oriented architecture (SOA). Instead of building large systems out of monolithic codebases, you were supposed to break problems down by creating separate services to manage each concern, and then create ways for those services to interact with each other as necessary, potentially to solve a wide array of problems with a single set of services.

In some ways, SOA was just an extension of the Unix design philosophy: do one thing, and do it well. A bash pipeline and an SOA-based system have more than a passing similarity. Unfortunately, many of the ideas behind SOA were easily perverted by enterprise software vendors, and we found ourselves talking about service buses, service discovery, SOAP, WSDLs, and lots of other horrible things. What we should have been focused on is how to make these services simpler and easier to access, not clever ways to organize and connect them.

The eighteenth century diplomat Charles Maurice de Talleyrand said, "An important art of politicians is to find new names for institutions which under old names have become odious to the public."[a] It's hard for me to think of microservices as anything but a reintroduction of SOA to a new generation of programmers who aren't scarred by the mistakes of the past. Maybe this time, we'll get it right.

---

a.   http://www.azquotes.com/author/14429-Charles_Maurice_de_Talleyrand

Adding Service Dependencies

As you build your own services, you're likely going to need to add libraries to support them. Any dependencies you need must be included in the code bundle, in the standard Node.js package directory, node_modules. To install the dependencies in our service, use the Node.js package manager, NPM.

The first dependency we're going to need is the AWS JavaScript SDK. It should already be included in the prepared workspace, and you can confirm this easily enough by checking the dependencies section of the package.json file, which looks like this:

learnjs/6000/services/package.json

```
{
  "name": "learnjs",
  "version": "1.0.0",
  "description": "learnjs",
  "main": "index.js",
  "scripts": {
    "test": "make test"
  },
  "author": "Ben Rady",
  "license": "All Rights Reserved",
  "dependencies": {
    "aws-sdk": "2.2.4"
  },
  "devDependencies": {
    "jasmine": "2.3.1"
  }
}
```

Run the sspa build_bundle command again to ensure you can install the dependencies. This command installs dependencies into the services/node_modules directory. When you build the deployment bundle, any dependencies in this directory are included, making them accessible to all your functions. Now that we've got the dependencies sorted out, it's time to write a test.

Building Testable Services

As with all the code in this application, our new Lambda function starts with a test. To write the tests for this function, we'll use the same testing framework we used in our single page app. However, as you'll see, we'll need to run the tests in a completely different environment.

The Jasmine testing framework is designed to work in both the browser and in headless environments like Node.js. Currently, one test in the prepared workspace tests the example echo function. Using the sspa command, you can run all the tests, like so:

```
learnjs $ ./sspa test
Started

.


1 spec, 0 failures
Finished in 0.005 seconds
```

Right now, our application services just have the one echo function and a single test. We'll want to add a new function and a describe section to hold the tests for it. When the service gets bigger, you'll want to pull everything apart into separate files, but for now, we can put the test in index_spec.js and the code in index.js. Let's take a look at a couple of the tests for this new function (with the surrounding context included).

learnjs/6302/services/spec/index_spec.js

```javascript
describe('lambda function', function() {
  var index = require('index');
  var context;

  beforeEach(function() {
    context = jasmine.createSpyObj('context', ['succeed', 'fail']);
    index.dynamodb = jasmine.createSpyObj('dynamo', ['scan']);
  });

  describe('popularAnswers', function() {
    it('requests problems with the given problem number', function() {
      index.popularAnswers({problemNumber: 42}, context);
      expect(index.dynamodb.scan).toHaveBeenCalledWith({
        FilterExpression: "problemId = :problemId",
        ExpressionAttributeValues: { ":problemId": 42 },
        TableName: 'learnjs'
      }, jasmine.any(Function));
    });

    it('groups answers by minified code', function() {
      index.popularAnswers({problemNumber: 1}, context);
      index.dynamodb.scan.calls.first().args[1](undefined, {Items: [
        {answer: "true"},
        {answer: "true"},
        {answer: "true"},
        {answer: "!false"},
        {answer: "!false"},
      ]});
      expect(context.succeed).toHaveBeenCalledWith({"true": 3, "!false": 2});
    });
  });
});
```

As you've seen with previous tests, you can stub out interactions with DynamoDB using a Jasmine spy object. You can test whether the service is using the right query parameters by making assertions about how methods on that object are called. By inspecting the calls to the scan method, you can invoke the callback passed in and simulate a response.

Make It 'til You Fake It

There's a quick way to see exactly what the real DynamoDB API returns in this case: don't fake out the interaction right away. The JavaScript AWS library will use the default credentials in your home directory (in ~/.aws/credentials) to actually make the request. When the request returns, you'll be able to see the real response right in your test output.

Keep in mind that this request is asynchronous, and you'll likely have to use the asynchronous test support in Jasmine, just as we did in *Asynchronous Testing with Jasmine,* on page 87. Also, remember that depending on what user the default credentials represent, you may have access to perform destructive operations, so be careful what services you use. Once you've seen how the API works, you'll want to fake out that interaction to keep your tests fast and reliable.

You can also create a fake context to use when invoking the Lambda function. Making assertions about what methods are called on this object, and what they're called with, will help you ensure your service is working properly. You can use this object to not only test the expected behavior of the Lambda function, but also to test to see how it handles failure conditions.

Querying, Grouping, and Paging

To implement our service function, we need to group the items by the answer attribute. DynamoDB doesn't have a built-in way to do a *group by* operation, but we can do it in our custom service (within some limits, as we'll see later). The tests assert that we perform the DynamoDB query and that the appropriate result is returned. If a failure occurs, we call the context.fail method to ensure that the function exits and the supplied error is logged.

Here, you'll see an implementation of this new service function that satisfies the tests in the previous section. You don't need to use this exact implementation in your app. In fact, you can improve upon it, as we'll discuss later, but this should give you an idea of what this service is supposed to do.

learnjs/6302/services/lib/index.js

```javascript
var http = require('http');
var AWS = require('aws-sdk');

AWS.config.region = 'us-east-1';

var config = {
  dynamoTableName: 'learnjs',
};

exports.dynamodb = new AWS.DynamoDB.DocumentClient();

function reduceItems(memo, items) {
  items.forEach(function(item) {
    memo[item.answer] = (memo[item.answer] || 0) + 1;
  });
  return memo;
}

function byCount(e1, e2) {
  return e2[0] - e1[0];
}

function filterItems(items) {
  var values = [];
  for (i in items) {
    values.push([items[i], i]);
  }
  var topFive = {};
  values.sort(byCount).slice(0,5).forEach(function(e) {
    topFive[e[1]] = e[0];
  })
  return topFive;
}

exports.popularAnswers = function(json, context) {
  exports.dynamodb.scan({
    FilterExpression: "problemId = :problemId",
    ExpressionAttributeValues: {
      ":problemId": json.problemNumber
    },
    TableName: config.dynamoTableName
  }, function(err, data) {
    if (err) {
      context.fail(err);
    } else {
      context.succeed(filterItems(reduceItems({}, data.Items)));
    }
  });
};

exports.echo = function(json, context) {
  context.succeed(["Hello from the cloud! You sent " + JSON.stringify(json)]);
};
```

This approach here works for small result sets, but it's a bit naive. To scale it up, we need to page through the scan results. The size limit for a query or scan request is 1MB of data. That means that if there is more than 1MB of answers in our app, the service we've created won't see them all.

DynamoDB responses include a LastEvaluatedKey field to allow us to page through results that are larger than 1MB.[5] By setting the ExclusiveStartKey property equal to the LastEvaluatedKey and resubmitting the request, we can page through the results in 1MB increments.

This allows our microservice to gather up the most popular answers without exceeding the DynamoDB response size limits. It also helps keep the memory footprint of our microservice small, which saves money.

To deploy this service, you need to run the deploy_bundle action with the sspa script, like so:

```
learnjs $ ./sspa deploy_bundle
```

This command runs the build_bundle command you ran earlier, and then takes the resulting code bundle and updates all the functions in our application using the lambda update-function-code command in the AWS CLI.

Once you've deployed the code, you should be ready to invoke this new service from our app. Rather than walking you through the process of building a new view for this service, as you saw in Chapter 3, *Essentials of Single Page Apps*, on page 45, we're going to skip right ahead to the good part...making the web service call.

Invoking Lambda Functions

You can invoke a Lambda function from a browser in two ways. The first way is to use the AWS SDK. The second is via the Amazon API Gateway. First, we're going to see how to invoke Lambda functions from the browser, using the AWS SDK and the Cognito credentials issued to the user.

By adding a new policy to our authenticated Cognito role, we can invoke Lambda functions directly from the browser without going through a public HTTP interface. As long as users have the proper credentials that let them assume the role, they can perform any operation listed in the policy. The particular operation we want to perform is named invoke. To perform this operation, you need to create an instance of the Lambda class from the AWS library. You then need to call the invoke function.

---

5. http://docs.aws.amazon.com/amazondynamodb/latest/developerguide/QueryAndScan.html#Pagination

Create a Lambda Policy

To allow access to this Lambda function, you need to create a new IAM policy and add it to the authorized Cognito role, just as we did in *Authorizing DynamoDB Access*, on page 103. Unlike that policy, you won't need a Condition clause in this one, because you're granting access to all authenticated users.

Of course, when using the Lambda API, we have the same issues with expiring credentials that we do with DynamoDB. Wouldn't it be great if we could reuse the sendDbRequest function to handle all that? Actually, we can…but you'll probably want to rename it to something like sendAwsRequest first. If the tests still pass once you've done that, you can go ahead and write a function to call the service.

`learnjs/6200/public/app.js`

```
learnjs.popularAnswers = function(problemId) {
  return learnjs.identity.then(function() {
    var lambda = new AWS.Lambda();
    var params = {
      FunctionName: 'learnjs_popularAnswers',
      Payload: JSON.stringify({problemNumber: problemId})
    };
    return learnjs.sendAwsRequest(lambda.invoke(params), function() {
      return learnjs.popularAnswers(problemId);
    });
  });
}
```

The tests for this new function follow the same patterns as the tests for our DynamoDB functions, so they're easy to write. Just as in the previous chapter, we're using jQuery Deferred objects to coordinate these requests. Adding this information into the views in our application takes much the same form.

One limitation of this approach is that only authenticated users will be able to make these requests. While it's possible to relax the permissions on this function and allow anyone to invoke it, there's another way to provide open access to this Lambda function so that anyone who wants to can invoke it. Next, we'll look at how to provide access to a Lambda function via Amazon's HTTP API Gateway.

Using the Amazon API Gateway

As we've seen, invoking Lambda functions via the AWS SDK with Cognito credentials can be a great way to integrate custom services into your applications, but what if you want to provide public access to a Lambda function?

You can make these functions accessible via an unauthenticated HTTP request using the Amazon API Gateway.

HTTP or HTTP?

While describing the API Gateway as "a way to invoke Lambda functions via HTTP" is correct, one thing to understand is that the AWS SDK for JavaScript *also* invokes Lambda functions via HTTP. Indeed, almost everything it does to interact with AWS is via HTTP, because that's the most stable protocol available from a web browser. It's just using a different endpoint than what's provided via the API Gateway.

The Amazon API Gateway maps *APIs* to Lambda functions through *endpoints* that you define with each function. You can create these APIs and their associated endpoints either through the Amazon API Gateway console or through the Lambda console. To create a public API for our function, we're going to use the Lambda console.

First, go to the settings page for our function in the Lambda console. Select the "API endpoints" tab, and click the "Add API endpoint" link. Once you do that, you'll be prompted to choose an endpoint type. Choose API Gateway, and you'll be presented with a configuration screen that looks like this:

Switch the security to Open, and don't mind the scary warning that shows up when you do. The whole point here is that we're trying to make this public. Next, switch the method to POST, because we want to use HTTP posts to deliver the request body. Set the deployment stage to either prod or test, depending on which version you're creating, and then pick an API name.

The API name is used to identify this API in the Gateway console. If you create lots of different applications using the same AWS account, you can use these names to differentiate APIs for different apps.

After saving these changes, you may have to wait a few seconds for them to be applied. Then you can try to make a request from the command line to ensure the API is active and publicly accessible. Get the endpoint URL from the Lambda console, and then using the curl command, make a POST request from the command line, like this:

```
$ curl -d '{"problemNumber":1}' «endpoint_url»
{"true":2,"!false":1}
```

If you get back a response like this, you know the service is working. You may get an empty JSON object if you haven't saved any answers. If you get a message that says "Missing Authentication Token," double-check your URL.

With that, we now have two methods for accessing this service: one authenticated method that uses the AWS JavaScript SDK and Cognito credentials, and a public HTTP API that anyone can access. Depending on the type of application that you're building, you may want to use one or both of these approaches.

Deploy Again

In this chapter, you learned how to build custom web services using Amazon Lambda. You saw two different methods for accessing these services and used them from two different environments (the command line and the browser). Since you've already deployed our new service, there's nothing more to do! If you want to try to integrate this new service into our app, you can experiment with some of the techniques we covered in previous chapters.

Next Steps

Now that you understand how Lambda works, here are some additional topics you might want to investigate.

Cognito User Validation

When creating a Cognito user pool, you can specify Lambda functions that are invoked when a user logs in or when a new user signs up. These functions can be used to validate user data before creating an account, to initialize database entries, or to send a custom confirmation message. User pools are a new addition to Cognito and offer more integration points than identity pools. See the Cognito documentation[6] for more details.

API Gateway

The API Gateway is also a new addition to Amazon Web Services, and its functionality is still growing. We saw one use of it in this chapter, but there are many others. For example, in addition to Lambda services, you can use Amazon EC2 as an endpoint. You can also use custom web services as endpoints. Keep an eye on this service,[7] and see if you can find other ways to use it.

Kappa, then Lambda

Kappa[8] is a command-line tool that automates some of the tasks we covered in this chapter. It creates IAM roles and Lambda functions, creates and deploys code bundles, and even lets you test your function with mock data, just as we did in the AWS console.

Deploying Lambda Functions to S3

Rather than updating the code for each individual function, you can deploy your code bundle to an S3 bucket. When all your code is contained in a single bundle, as ours is, this can make a lot of sense. See the AWS documentation for more details.[9]

---

6.   http://docs.aws.amazon.com/cognito/latest/
7.   https://aws.amazon.com/api-gateway/
8.   https://github.com/garnaat/kappa
9.   https://blogs.aws.amazon.com/application-management/post/Tx3TPMTH0EVGA64/Automatically-Deploy-from-Amazon-S3-using-AWS-CodeDeploy

CHAPTER 7

Serverless Security

Building secure software systems is hard. One of the things that makes it hard is that it's difficult to know when you've got it right. Conversely, it's sometimes embarrassingly easy to figure out if you've got it wrong: just put your service on the Internet, wait, and pay attention.

In this chapter, we're going to start by reviewing some basic rules for keeping your AWS account secure. Then we'll spend the rest of the chapter examining some common attacks that can be used against serverless web applications. We'll see how attacks work and what we can do to prevent them. Hopefully, by understanding the specifics of these attacks, you'll be able to see the vulnerabilities in your own applications and find ways to make them secure.

> Anyone can invent a security system that he himself cannot break....When someone hands you a security system and says, "I believe this is secure," the first thing you have to ask is, "Who the hell are you?" Show me what you've broken to demonstrate that your assertion of the system's security means something.

— Bruce Schneier, cryptography researcher and author

Securing Your AWS Account

The first step in securing your application is making sure your AWS account is secure. No application safeguards in the world will be effective if an attacker can just log into your AWS account and turn them off.

In fact, if your AWS account becomes compromised, more than just a single application would be at risk. Accidentally allowing an attacker to access your AWS account can be an expensive mistake. Anyone who gains access to it could, for example, spin up hundreds of *g2.8xlarge* EC2 instances and mine for bitcoins until you discover what's going on. There have been cases of people writing bots to check public GitHub accounts for AWS credentials to do this very thing. So before we talk about application security, we're going to cover the basics of AWS account security.

Disabling Any Root Access Keys

If you've created root access keys for your account, you should delete them. You cannot manage these keys like keys for regular IAM users, and you have fewer options available to you should you need to revoke the keys or retroactively restrict what services they're allowed to access.

If you haven't created these kinds of access keys already, don't. They can't do anything that you can't do with an IAM user with administrative privileges. The advantage of IAM users is that you can always restrict those privileges later without completely disabling the key. That means if you've deployed a script, app, or tool that uses those keys, you can easily fine-tune the access over time if you find that you've granted more access than you should have.

Managing Users with Profiles

In *Creating an AWS User with Access Keys*, on page 16, we created an AWS user with administrative privileges. This user has complete access to everything in your account, which makes doing things like creating tables and services easy. However, this level of access means you might want to take some extra precautions when managing the access keys for this user, to guard against using them accidentally.

One way to keep these credentials safe is to use separate profiles that provide different levels of access. The sspa script uses the *admin* profile to keep those credentials from accidentally being used in unexpected ways—interacting with the AWS SDK for JavaScript when running tests for the Lambda services, for example, which uses those default credentials unless you tell it not to.

The profile option we added when running aws configure back in Chapter 1 told AWS CLI to add the credentials to the admin profile. The sspa script uses this --profile option again whenever it runs commands to interact with AWS.

Securing AWS Credentials

Another way to keep credentials safe is to keep them in a secure location. By default, the AWS CLI writes its configuration files to your home directory, and these files are not encrypted. Anyone who gains physical access to your computer could read those files. This can happen in unexpected ways. If you give an old computer to a friend, who then sells it when he buys a replacement, your hard drive could wind up in anyone's hands. If your keys files are still on that drive, you could be in for a large AWS bill.

A simple counter to the problem is to ensure those files are encrypted. Some operating systems offer encrypted filesystems as a way to prevent these kinds of problems. OS X can encrypt your entire hard drive with a feature called FileVault,[1] while Ubuntu has EncryptedHome, which mounts an encrypted partition in your home directory.[2] Windows also offers a mechanism to encrypt folders on the filesystem.[3]

With an encrypted folder, you can move the files to the encrypted directory and then create a symlink at the original location, so that the AWS CLI can read the files when the encrypted directory has been mounted. If your entire drive is encrypted, as is the case with FileVault, then no additional steps are necessary.

Set Up Multifactor Authentication

For an extra layer of security, you can require that people trying to authenticate as a user under your account supply a generated security code in addition to a password or other credentials. You can use a number of compatible apps and devices to generate these codes, which are temporary and rotate every sixty seconds. This is commonly called *multifactor authentication*, or MFA.

Options for mobile devices include the Google Authenticator app[4] (which supports third-party accounts like AWS), the Authy app,[5] and Amazon's own Virtual MFA app,[6] which works on Android devices. In addition, you can get a physical key fob[7] from Amazon for $12.99.

Adding MFA is an especially good idea for your AWS account, but you can also use it with IAM users within your account. For users who have administrative privileges but have credentials that must be stored in plain text (for one reason or another) and are used interactively, this can be a great way to prevent a breach.

Now that we've got the basics of account security down, let's look at some specific attacks that serverless apps might be vulnerable to. We'll dig into

---

1. https://support.apple.com/en-us/HT204837
2. https://help.ubuntu.com/community/EncryptedHome
3. http://windows.microsoft.com/en-us/windows/encrypt-decrypt-folder-file#1TC=windows-7
4. https://itunes.apple.com/us/app/google-authenticator/id388497605?mt=8
5. https://www.authy.com/
6. http://www.amazon.com/gp/product/B0061MU68M
7. http://onlinenoram.gemalto.com/

what makes these attacks work and what you can do to prevent them. By the end of the chapter, you should have a good sense of the kind of attacks your serverless single page apps might face.

Query Injection Attacks

The first type of attack we're going to look at is a *query injection attack*. You may have heard of a more specific type of this attack: a SQL injection attack. But this particular attack vector can take many forms, and not all of them are based on SQL.

Part of the custom service we created in the previous chapter makes a DynamoDB scan request. In that request, we used the ExpressionAttributeValues parameter to add parameterized values to the query. The FilterExpression string referred to these values. Take another look at that code, and see if anything seems strange to you:

learnjs/7000/services/lib/index.js

```
exports.dynamodb.scan({
  FilterExpression: "problemId = :problemId",
  ExpressionAttributeValues: {
    ":problemId": json.problemNumber
  },
  TableName: config.dynamoTableName
```

When looking at this code, you might wonder why we didn't just append the problemNumber attribute value directly into the FilterExpression string. Why bother creating a :problemId expression variable only to use it once? Wouldn't just building the query string be simpler?

Unlike the DynamoDB requests that we run from the browser, nothing in the IAM policy for our Lambda function restricts access to any data in the table. So if a user submits a request with a problemId that is actually a partial expression clause, it would be appended onto the end of the expression. Since we're counting on that expression to limit access to only specific records, that could create a breach. For example, this request would return all the records in the database:

```
$ curl -d '{"problemNumber":'1 OR problemId > 0'}' «endpoint_url»
```

The following request would return all the records belonging to a user with the CognitoID abc123:

```
$ curl -d '{"problemNumber":'1 OR userId = abc123'}' «endpoint_url»
```

As you can see, manually constructing the query string for a database request can lead to all kinds of problems, whether you're using a SQL database or not. By writing the query using variable names and letting DynamoDB insert the values for us, we can prevent an injection attack. Using the ExpressionAttributeValues field in our request ensures that submitting a query like the previous ones will either raise an error or simply return no results, because there are no records where the problemId attribute is the string "1 OR problemId > 0".

The next attack we'll look at is similar in form. But rather than injecting a query text in a service, we're going to see how an attacker can inject JavaScript in a browser.

Cross-Site Scripting Attacks

A *cross-site scripting* (XSS) attack involves including <script> tags or other HTML markup in content that is appended directly to HTML elements in a page. This causes the markup to be evaluated, and in the case of <script> tags, this means that the JavaScript inside the tags will be evaluated. Since single page apps make heavy use of dynamic HTML, we need to be concerned about this kind of attack.

XSS Injection Methods

In 2014, programmer Jamie Hankins demonstrated a flaw in many websites that provide DNS information. DNS records are public and free to access, so many sites have sprung up to let people easily find this information on the web. Unfortunately, some of these sites are hastily constructed, and they found themselves a victim of this funny and enlightening prank.

By updating the DNS records for his personal domain to include JavaScript tags, Hankins was able to get many of these sites to dance to the Harlem Shake, playing music and moving the page elements around to the beat.[8] While this particular attack only affected people looking up DNS information for his website, it exposed a glaring and potentially dangerous bug...and was hilarious.

In our application right now, we have untrusted data that could be a potential vector for this kind of attack. The answer attribute on our DynamoDB records is ideally supposed to be a correct answer, but there is no guarantee that it is. The application logic checks for this, of course, but this is purely a convenience for the user. Anyone who wanted to could write an answer record using

---

8. http://www.tomsguide.com/us/harlem-shake-hack,news-19595.html

their own Cognito ID that didn't contain a correct answer…or didn't contain JavaScript at all.

Because of this, we have to be careful with what we do with this data. For example, when building a view to display it, you would want to make sure to use jQuery's text() method to set the text of an element that would show it. This method creates a text node in the DOM that escapes HTML tags and other special characters so that it can be safely added to the page. Using other methods like append or prepend would cause any unsafe markup to be added as is, creating an XSS vulnerability.

Sandboxing JavaScript Using Web Workers

Right now, our app suffers from a sort of self-imposed XSS attack. Because users' answers are evaluated in the same context as the application, the code the users enter can interfere with the application itself. While this isn't a security problem, per se, it can create some very strange behavior. Take a look at this perfectly reasonable (if not a tad verbose) answer to problem #1:

```
learnjs = true;
return learnjs;
```

Because this code is missing the var keyword when declaring the learnjs variable, running this code in the context of our app will overwrite our application namespace, causing an error like this:

```
Uncaught TypeError: learnjs.buildCorrectFlash is not a function
```

To prevent user code from interfering with our application, we can evaluate users' answers in a *web worker*. A web worker runs in a separate thread from the main application, and you communicate with it by posting and receiving messages. Creating a web worker to evaluate our users' answers will allow us to isolate that code from the rest of our app.

To create a web worker, you first need to create a separate JavaScript file that specifies the worker behavior. This worker file needs to assign a function to a global onmessage variable that will be invoked whenever the worker receives a message. The function will be invoked with an event object that can contain data we want to pass to the worker.

All the worker function needs to do is evaluate the answer and post a response. If an exception is raised, it can simply respond with false. Create a new file in the public directory named worker.js, and add this function to it:

learnjs/7100/public/worker.js

```javascript
onmessage = function(e) {
  try {
    postMessage(eval(e.data));
  } catch(e) {
    postMessage(false);
  }
}
```

Once you've created the worker file, you can integrate it into the app. To do this, you need to change the behavior of the checkAnswer function you created back in Chapter 3. This function should use the web worker to evaluate a user's answer. Since this process will be asynchronous, you can return a jQuery Deferred to allow the Check Answer button's click handler to update the UI once the answer has been evaluated. The result should look something like this:

learnjs/7100/public/app.js

```javascript
function checkAnswer() {
  var def = $.Deferred();
  var test = problemData.code.replace('__', answer.val()) + '; problem();';
  var worker = new Worker('worker.js');
  worker.onmessage = function(e) {
    if (e.data) {
      def.resolve(e.data);
    } else {
      def.reject();
    }
  }
  worker.postMessage(test);
  return def;
}
```

Here, we're using the postMessage method on the worker to send the user's answer, wrapped in a JavaScript function. Note the onmessage handler function that is set on the worker to receive the response.

learnjs/7100/public/app.js

```javascript
function checkAnswerClick() {
  checkAnswer().done(function() {
    var flashContent = learnjs.buildCorrectFlash(problemNumber);
    learnjs.flashElement(resultFlash, flashContent);
    learnjs.saveAnswer(problemNumber, answer.val());
  }).fail(function() {
    learnjs.flashElement(resultFlash, 'Incorrect!');
  });
  return false;
}
```

Cross-site scripting attacks are sometimes the first in a series of steps designed to compromise an application. Not only can injected scripts read or change any resources accessible in the browser, but they can also submit authenticated requests to web services that store credentials as cookies. This second technique is called *cross-site request forgery*, and it's the next attack on our web security naughty list.

Cross-Site Request Forgery

Cross-site request forgery (XSRF) involves using credentials stored in the browser to make authenticated requests to web services. Often combined with an XSS attack, these types of attacks allow malicious JavaScript to impersonate you, performing actions without your knowledge or consent.

This attack requires a web service to store authentication tokens in the browser, either in browser cookies or in the application layer. How these tokens are accessed depends on how they're stored. Cookie-based tokens are simply added to any matching outgoing request, so all an attacker has to do is make a valid request, and the authentication information will be added by the browser. Attacks against application-layer tokens require that the attacker either know where the tokens are stored or know how to use JavaScript to make a request that will include those tokens.

Understanding Cookies

When you make a request to a website, the response from the site can optionally include the Set-Cookie HTTP header. The text of this header includes a value or key-value pair, and it can include metadata like an expiration date, path, and domain options. Here's an example:

```
Set-Cookie: sessionToken=sessionID_abc123; Expires=Fri, 13 Feb 2009 23:31:30 GMT
```

The options set on the cookie (like Expires) come into play whenever the browser makes a request back to the site that previously returned a response with the Set-Cookie header. Any cookies that are still valid and match the properties of the request (like the domain and path) are sent back to the server. All previously received cookies are sent as the value of a single request header named Cookie, like so:

```
Cookie: otherCookie=yes; sessionToken=sessionID_abc123
```

By setting and receiving cookies, web services can store state for an individual user in that user's browser. Sometimes, the data in a cookie is encrypted to prevent inspection of the data by the users or by third parties. This is often the case when cookies are used to store authentication tokens.

XSRF Without Javascript

While JavaScript seems to be an obvious choice for an XSRF attack, sometimes it's possible to do without it. Although they don't conform with the conventions of HTTP, some web services provide APIs that allow you to perform requests that have side effects using HTTP GET requests. In these cases, injecting an <img> or other resource tag onto the page is enough to make the request.

It's also possible to create an HTTP POST request without JavaScript. By injecting a hidden HTML form onto the page, you can trick the browser into sending a POST request containing that form data. This requires that the service accept form-encoded data in the POST body.

In our application, any malicious code injected into our app could easily perform an XSRF attack by interacting with the AWS JavaScript SDK, our application, or both. Thankfully, the AWS APIs we use in our app use proper HTTP semantics and require a POST to perform any operation that changes data. You should take care to follow these conventions when building custom web services as well. Creating a service that changes data in response to an HTTP GET can open your application up to XSRF attacks.

Cross-Origin Requests and the Same-Origin Policy

One thing that can prevent basic XSRF attacks is the *same-origin* policy, enforced by all modern browsers. This policy restricts access to resources that come from a different *origin* on the web. The origin is a combination of the URI[9] scheme, the hostname, and the port number. For example, all of these URLs refer to different origins, even though they might actually all connect to the same server:

1. http://example.com

2. http://www.example.com

3. https://www.example.com

4. http://www.example.com:8080

Not only do browsers use the same-origin policy to segregate cookies from different sites, but by default they also prevent HTTP requests with side effects (POST, PUT, and DELETE) from being sent to sites with different origins than the one of the page currently loaded. That means that if you load an app using the URL http://learnjs.benrady.com and you try to make a POST request to http://www.google.com, the browser will block that request.

---

9. https://en.wikipedia.org/wiki/Uniform_Resource_Identifier#Syntax

Cross-Origin Resource Sharing

If you want to allow access to information across different origins, you can use cross-origin resource sharing (CORS) headers to do it. The web service responding to the request needs to add the Access-Control-Allow-Origin headers on the response to tell the browser to permit the request.

You might be wondering how adding a header to the *response* helps here, since at that point, the request has already been accepted and processed. Well, to address this issue, browsers will issue a *preflight*[a] OPTIONS request before attempting the actual request, to see if the web service returns a CORS header or not. If the current origin matches the value returned on the header, the browser sends the original request to the service. If not, the request is blocked.

---

a.   https://en.wikipedia.org/wiki/Cross-origin_resource_sharing#Preflight_example

Back in Chapter 4, *Identity as a Service with Amazon Cognito*, on page 71, when we created an application in the Google Developers Console, we had to specify the origins that were allowed to access the Google API on behalf of our application. By requiring that we specify these origins, Google helps prevent XSRF attacks in our application.

Now that we've seen how our application can fall victim to some protocol and application-level attacks, let's drop down a couple of layers and look at how the security of the network transport affects our application. While you might not deal with this layer of technology often, understanding how to send data securely and privately over the Internet is an essential part of building secure web applications.

Wire Attacks and Transport Layer Security

When you send data over the Internet, you should have no expectation that it is kept secret. Every packet sent is like a tiny postcard, and anyone along the way who wants to bother to look can do so. This inherent transparency of the Internet makes Transport Layer Security (TLS) one of the fundamental security technologies of the web.

 HTTPS is the HTTP protocol over TLS or SSL.

Along with its predecessor, the Secure Sockets Layer (SSL) standard, TLS provides a way to negotiate a secure, encrypted channel of communication. It also allows the communicating parties to verify their identity by using

public key cryptography. Every time you look in your browser windows and see a little lock icon telling you that your requests are being encrypted and sent to the right place, you have TLS to thank. It's critical, therefore, to consider all the HTTP requests your application makes, and check that they're using TLS to ensure the security of your users' data.

Sidejacking Attacks

For example, using HTTPS for only *some* parts of an application can create serious problems. Apps that log users in using HTTPS but then issue identity tokens that are transmitted in plain text are vulnerable to *sidejacking* attacks. These attacks allow a third party to impersonate the user and make requests on their behalf while the identity token remains valid. Such attacks can be hard to detect.

In 2010, a sidejacking exploit for Facebook was released as a browser plugin for Firefox. Named Firesheep, it brought much-needed attention to an extant security problem. While Facebook logins were protected by HTTPS, interaction with the site was not, so anyone could grab an authorization token from an unprotected request and then impersonate that user until the token expired.

In 2013, possibly as a result of the wide publicity generated by Firesheep and other exploits, Facebook made TLS the default access method for all users. Many other sites have followed suit, and in many circles, HTTPS is now considered the default method of communication on the web.

Using HTTPS Effectively

Currently, our app only uses HTTPS for *some* communication. Is this a problem? To find out, we're going to walk through our application step by step and find out what parts are secure and what parts are not.

The application itself is not loaded using HTTPS. The http URL that you use to access it should be the first indication. This isn't really an issue, however, because the app is supposed to be publicly accessible. It contains no sensitive data, and there's no way for our users to add any data to the static files we have hosted in S3.

It's possible that HTTPS would provide some privacy for our users, preventing a third party from seeing what parts of our app they're using. In countries with poor civil rights records, this can be a big concern. Since our entire app is loaded at once, not as the user navigates through the app, there isn't a lot of information to be gained from spying on this traffic. The only way to be sure, would be to encrypt the communication by serving the app over HTTPS.

Unencrypted traffic can reveal usage patterns of public websites.

Our application's sign-in process uses Google's OAuth2 endpoint.[10] Looking at this request in the browser's Network tab, you can see that this endpoint is served using HTTPS. Similarly, the requests we make to create a Cognito identity and request temporary AWS credentials are also served over HTTPS.

All Amazon Web Services APIs are accessible through TLS-protected endpoints. We just need to ensure that we're using the right endpoints. Since we're connecting to these services using the JavaScript SDK, we'll need to use it to configure how our application connects to AWS. DynamoDB uses a secure connection by default, but we can disable this by setting the sslEnabled option to false. You could configure this in the same parameters object where you set the region, but why would you want to do that?

Using Wireshark

One reason you might want to turn off encryption is to be able to see your application's requests and responses at the network level. Similarly, a great way to know *for sure* that your app isn't sending data in plain text is to inspect it yourself. Wireshark[a] is a tool that shows you, packet by packet, what your application is sending over the network. It has sophisticated analysis tools that can reassemble TCP conversations and filter traffic by source, destination, protocol, or any of hundreds of other criteria.

a.   https://www.wireshark.org/

Lastly, when our app invokes Lambda functions using the AWS SDK, you can see those requests are made using HTTPS. The exact endpoint used for the request depends on the region where the Lambda service resides. You can see the specific endpoint for your region by examining the request in the Network tab. The public URL we use to access our Lambda service through the API Gateway is also protected by HTTPS.

At this point, we can be reasonably confident that all the sensitive data in our application is protected in transit by HTTPS. We've verified that all the network requests our app makes use HTTPS, with the exception of the application load, which doesn't contain user information. Next, we're going to look at a type of attack that can really cost you...literally.

---

10. https://accounts.google.com

Denial-of-Service Attacks

A *denial-of-service* (DoS) attack allows an attacker to overwhelm a traditional web application with malformed network traffic, intentionally slow clients, or lots and lots of requests. With just a basic understanding of how an app works, an attacker could create much more work for the app than it can handle, bringing one or more application tiers to a crashing halt and preventing any users from using the app. This attack can be performed at the TCP packet layer, at the HTTP protocol layer, or at the application request layer. No matter what layer is being attacked, asymmetry between the work required to create a request and the work required to handle it makes a DoS attack feasible and effective.

Because our app is built on top of AWS, we have a different problem. Rather than crashing the application, it's much more likely that an attacker could cause our app to rack up lots of computing costs, resulting in a nasty surprise when we get your AWS bill at the end of the month. To prevent this from happening, we have to look at the various parts of our app and see what we can do to protect them.

Protecting S3 with CloudFront

Perhaps the most essential behavior we need to safeguard in the face of a DoS attack is the ability for users to load our app. Once our application is loaded, we have a world of options available to mitigate an ongoing attack, but if the application never loads in a user's browser, all is lost. One way to ensure our app will load successfully, even when being attacked, is to serve the app's static content stored in S3 using *Amazon CloudFront.*

Aside from simply functioning as a content delivery service, Amazon has some protections baked into CloudFront that detect and mitigate DoS attacks (although the company doesn't like to talk about it).[11] Since our app is just a bunch of static content served to the browser, we can take advantage of these protections by using CloudFront to provide access to our app.

To set up CloudFront, create a new *distribution*, which controls how the content is cached, where the content is sourced, and how access to the content is logged. This process is straightforward and well documented in the AWS docs.[12] Choose the Restrict Bucket Access option, as we don't want attackers to be able to circumvent CloudFront and access the S3 bucket directly.

---

11. https://forums.aws.amazon.com/message.jspa?messageID=253609
12. http://docs.aws.amazon.com/gettingstarted/latest/swh/getting-started-create-cfdist.html

Once the distribution is created, you need to change the CNAME DNS entry you created back in Chapter 1 to point to the CloudFront endpoint. That endpoint will look something like d707s2ze1o682.cloudfront.net. Unless you take steps to temporarily allow direct S3 access, the site may be unavailable while the DNS change is propagating. Once the DNS change takes effect, our app will be served through CloudFront.

Creating a CloudFront distribution will not only help protect our app from DoS attacks, but will also provide faster access to users. There are dozens of CloudFront *edge locations*[13] around the world, providing local access to your application users in that region.

Distributed Denial-of-Service

In order to make their attacks harder to thwart, Internet ne'er-do-wells usually launch DoS attacks from multiple places simultaneously. Harmful requests originating from a single IP address can usually be detected easily and blocked using either a hardware or software firewall. Requests coming from a seemingly random set of IP addresses are harder to deal with. Such an attack is referred to as a *distributed denial-of-service attack* (DDoS).

Scalable Services and User Identities

Attacking DynamoDB and Lambda with a DoS attack is more difficult, but not impossible. To do it, attackers need to create Cognito identities that they can use to make requests; otherwise, those requests are denied.

Cognito, DynamoDB, and Lambda are relatively new technologies, so it's hard to say what types of attacks are likely. One can imagine a potential application-level attack that would involve creating a throwaway user with an identity provider such as Google, and then filling up our DynamoDB table with bogus records created by that user.

To detect such an attack, we could use Amazon's CloudWatch service to set up alarms to notify us about unusual usage patterns. For example, a Cloud-Watch alarm on the number of DynamoDB writes might help us detect this type of attack. We'll cover CloudWatch in depth in the next chapter.

Assuming that we can detect the attack when it happens, what can we do about it? Once thing we can do is change the Condition clause in the IAM policy that grants Cognito users access to DynamoDB or Lambda. Specifically,

---

13. https://aws.amazon.com/cloudfront/details/

excluding the user identity that's responsible for creating all the bogus records would prevent the attacker from writing any new ones. The attacker would have to create another identity with an identity provider before resuming the attack.

Deploy Again

In this chapter, we looked at some of the different kinds of attacks that you can encounter when building serverless single page apps. While there are no silver bullets when it comes to security, the more you understand the likely threats, the better equipped you'll be to deal with them if and when they happen.

If you haven't already done so, go ahead and deploy the web worker change we added earlier in the chapter. This should help prevent strange interactions between our users' JavaScript answers and our app.

Next Steps

Now that you understand some of the common attacks against serverless web applications, here are some additional topics you might want to investigate. To keep things simple, I haven't expanded on them in the book, but you might want to explore them on your own before moving on to the next chapter.

Using Signed URLs

Using the AWS SDK, you can generate signed URLs that provide temporary access to restricted files and other resources. You can store these resources in S3 and cache them using CloudFront. See the AWS docs for more details.[14]

Defeating DDoS

Although we touched on the topic in this chapter, defending against DDoS attacks is a deep topic. For a more complete explanation of how to defend your application against these kinds of attacks while running in AWS, check out the Amazon whitepaper "AWS Best Practices for DDoS Resiliency.[15]

In the next chapter, we're going to see what happens when our app gets popular. We'll project the cost of running the app as it scales up to millions of users, and we'll look at some of the tools we can use to monitor our app as it grows.

---

14. http://docs.aws.amazon.com/AmazonCloudFront/latest/DeveloperGuide/private-content-signed-urls.html
15. https://d0.awsstatic.com/whitepapers/DDoS_White_Paper_June2015.pdf

CHAPTER 8

Scaling Up

Our application now delivers on its basic promise: answering JavaScript programming puzzles. Are we ready to share it with the world?

Let's say we share it with friends, who share it with their friends, and so on. Eventually, millions of people are using the app. How will it perform? What will it cost to support all of these users? How will we monitor it when it's performing thousands of operations a day?

You might not start thinking about these problems until an app has exceeded your wildest dreams. They're good problems to have, but they're still problems. In this chapter, you're going to see some potential solutions to these problems and learn how to apply them. That way, when your application grows into the millions of users, you'll be ready to take action.

Monitor Web Services

Much like parenting a child, you'll want to watch your application grow, succeed, and sometimes...fail. Otherwise, you might not realize what it's doing until it's too late! Application monitoring for a serverless app takes a different form than a traditional application, because it has no application server to act as a central access point of information. That doesn't mean we're at any disadvantage; it just means that we need to do things differently.

As a first step, we need to monitor the web services we're using. To do that, we can use...another web service! Amazon's *CloudWatch* service lets us monitor and send alerts based on statistics provided by both Amazon Web Services and any custom services we run.

CloudWatch is a service that provides monitoring and notifications on both AWS and user-defined metrics. CloudWatch has built-in support for many AWS services, and monitoring statistics for these services is usually as easy as clicking a few buttons in the CloudWatch console or running an AWS CLI command. It also provides an API that you can use to send your own statistics and log messages. Whether you care about built-in or user-defined metrics, when one of your stats exceeds a threshold, you can send email alerts to an address you specify.

Monitor Your Capacity Limits

If you remember back to *Provisioned Throughput*, on page 100, we specified the read and write capacity limit for our DynamoDB table. The first question you might have after setting these limits is, "How do I know when I've gone over the limit?" Without some sort of monitoring on this service, aside from angry complaints from users, you'll have no way to know.

Thankfully, we can create a CloudWatch alarm that will alert us if any requests to DynamoDB fail because our capacity limits have been exceeded. But before we create the alarm, we need to create a place for the alert to go. With CloudWatch, you have two options: you can send the alert to Amazon's *Simple Notification Service* (SNS) or an Amazon Auto Scaling policy. We just want to be notified of this event and not change any settings automatically, so let's send this alert to an SNS topic.

You may be wondering what the heck SNS is. Do we really have to bring yet another web service into this? Why not just send a text or email? Well, you can do both of those things, and more, from SNS. Also called the Push Notification service, SNS allows you to create *topics* that can receive notifications and publish them to multiple *subscriptions*. Subscriptions can handle these notifications via different protocols, such as email, text messages, or an HTTP POST (sometimes called a webhook). Perhaps not surprisingly, you can even send these notification into Amazon's Simple Queue Service (SQS),[1] or a Lambda microservice if you want to consume them programmatically.

Although the configuration options might be a bit overwhelming, Amazon is giving us a lot of flexibility on how to handle this alert by sending it into SNS. But this means the first step in creating our alarm is setting up this SNS topic. We can do that with the AWS command-line interface, just as we have been using for our other services. The command we need is sns create-topic, and you can use it like this:

```
$ aws --profile admin sns create-topic --name EmailAlerts
```

---

1. https://aws.amazon.com/sqs/

Peeling Back the Curtain

In the previous chapters, we used the sspa script to interact with AWS to create DynamoDB tables, IAM policies, and other resources. Under the covers, this script uses the AWS CLI to perform these operations.

In this chapter, rather than using the sspa script to interact with AWS, I'm going to show you how to use the AWS CLI more directly. Most of the things we'll do in this chapter are pretty simple, so it's a good place to introduce this tool. As you get more comfortable with it, you can go back and look at the sspa script to see what it was doing for you earlier in the book.

This command returns the ARN of the topic, which we'll need for the next few steps, so keep track of it. Once you create the topic, you can add a *subscription* that will send an email, using the sns subscribe command and giving it a protocol and email address, like so:

```
$ aws --profile admin sns subscribe \
    --topic-arn «your_topic_arn» \
    --protocol email \
    --notification-endpoint you@example.com
```

Running this command causes an email to be sent immediately to the address you specify. This email contains a confirmation link that you need to click to enable the subscription. Once that's complete, we're ready to send alerts to this topic. To configure the new CloudWatch alarm, you can use the cloudwatch put-metric-alarm command in the AWS command-line interface. Here's an example of an alarm you could create:

```
$ aws --profile admin cloudwatch put-metric-alarm \
    --actions-enabled \
    --alarm-name 'DynamoDB Capacity' \
    --comparison-operator GreaterThanOrEqualToThreshold \
    --evaluation-periods 1 \
    --metric-name ThrottledRequests \
    --namespace AWS/DynamoDB \
    --period 60 \
    --statistic Sum \
    --threshold 1 \
    --alarm-action «your_topic_arn»
```

This alarm watches a DynamoDB metric named ThrottledRequests, which measures the number of requests to DynamoDB that failed because the apps didn't have sufficient provisioned capacity. The other options in this command specify that the alarm samples the data over a single sixty-second period, taking the sum of all the data points in that one period. If the number of failed requests is greater than or equal to the threshold of one, then the alarm is triggered. That causes a notification to be sent to the SNS topic we just created, specified in the alarm-action option. If you receive an alert, you'll probably want to look at the query usage patterns in the app, then raise the capacity limit accordingly.

Being notified when a problem occurs is helpful, but what would be even better is if we could be notified *before* problems start to happen. Thankfully, there are other DynamoDB metrics you can monitor. For example, by checking the ConsumedReadCapacityUnits and ConsumedWriteCapacityUnits metrics, you can trigger this alarm if the application exceeds a portion of its allocated capacity...say, eighty percent. This can help you anticipate capacity problems before they start causing database operations to fail.

 Amazon limits you to four throughput capacity changes per UTC calendar day.

One thing to recognize is that this alert is *global*—that is, it will trigger an alert if this metric is exceeded on any DynamoDB table. To limit this alert to just our production table for LearnJS, we need to add a *dimension* using the dimensions option for the cloudwatch put-metric-alarm command. Dimensions allow you to limit an alarm to certain resources or operations, and most of the DynamoDB metrics allow you to specify a TableName dimension when creating an alarm. See the DynamoDB metrics documentation for details.[2]

Creating Billing Alerts

In addition to monitoring the performance of the web services in your application, you can measure the performance of your credit card. By setting up a billing alarm with CloudWatch, you can check every hour to see if your estimated AWS charges exceed a threshold. Getting that alert will help you take action before you wind up with a huge bill at the end of the month. Here's an example of how to create such an alarm:

```
$ aws --profile admin cloudwatch put-metric-alarm \
    --alarm-name 'Billing Alarm' \
    --comparison-operator GreaterThanOrEqualToThreshold \
    --dimensions "Name=Currency,Value=USD" \
    --evaluation-periods 1 \
    --metric-name EstimatedCharges \
```

2. http://docs.aws.amazon.com/amazondynamodb/latest/developerguide/MonitoringDynamoDB.html#dynamodb-metrics

```
--namespace AWS/Billing \
--period 3600 \
--statistic Maximum \
--threshold 100 \
--actions-enabled \
--alarm-actions «your_topic_arn»
```

The threshold we're using for this alarm is $100. It can reuse the same email notification SNS topic we used for our other alert. Unlike the AWS/DynamoDB namespace, EstimatedCharges is (currently) the only metric you can monitor in the AWS/Billing namespace...but feel free to check the documentation[3] for updates.

Unexpected Expenses

If you do wake up one morning to find that your billing alerts have been tripped and that you racked up a huge AWS bill overnight, don't panic. After turning down or turning off whatever services have been going haywire, contact Amazon for help.[a] Depending on the cause, it may be able to reduce or eliminate any unexpected charges and work with you to prevent these kinds of errors in the future.

Amazon wants to keep you as a happy customer, and it's often willing to help when things go wrong. AWS is not a con game to trick you into spending a bunch of money all at once by making a mistake, suffering from someone else's mistake, or being the victim of an online attack. Amazon wants you to use its services month after month and be satisfied with the results you're getting for your money.

a.   https://aws.amazon.com/contact-us/

In addition to these two examples, you can set up alarms for many different services and metrics in AWS. You can create new SNS topics to send notifications via more immediate methods, such as a text message. You can also create custom services to consume the notifications programmatically to take action automatically when a limit is exceeded. You can find the complete list of metrics and namespaces in the AWS documentation.[4]

Analyze S3 Web Traffic

So we've got a great way to monitor the web services that we're using, but we still need a way to see what the application itself is doing. In a traditional web app, we would normally front our application server with a dedicated web

---

3.   http://docs.aws.amazon.com/AmazonCloudWatch/latest/DeveloperGuide/billing-metricscollected.html

4.   http://docs.aws.amazon.com/AmazonCloudWatch/latest/DeveloperGuide/CW_Support_For_AWS.html

server, like Apache or Nginx. In addition to other tasks, this web server could provide access logs that we could use to monitor our traffic.

Of course, using the traditional approach, you also need a way to aggregate those logs from all of your web servers as you scale horizontally. Because we're using Amazon S3 to host our app, we don't have that problem. However, the logs that S3 produces are a little different than the kinds of logs created by a traditional web server, so we're going to take a look at them and see some common techniques for extracting useful data.

Logging S3 Requests

As we saw in Chapter 1, *Starting Simple*, on page 1, you can use an Amazon S3 bucket as a static web host, which is what we're doing for our app. Amazon provides a facility in S3 to log all the web requests made to that bucket. To do this, you need to create another S3 bucket and then configure the web bucket to write logs to that other bucket. You can then download the logs from the S3 bucket, or build other analysis tools that access them directly.

To configure the bucket, we're going to use the s3api put-bucket-logging command in the AWS CLI. But first, we need to create a bucket to place our logs in and grant S3 permission to write to it. The sspa create_bucket command we used before will configure the bucket as a web host, so instead you can use the AWS CLI s3 mb command, like so:

```
$ aws --profile admin s3 mb s3://learnjs-logging.benrady.com
make_bucket: s3://learnjs-logging.benrady.com
```

Note that since you're not following this up with the s3 website command, this bucket will not serve its contents via HTTP (which is a good thing). Next, we need to grant write access to our bucket. Amazon S3 will write the log files to this bucket as a member of the predefined *Log Delivery* Amazon S3 group. To allow this, you must enable the appropriate access control restrictions on the bucket using the s3api put-bucket-acl in AWS CLI. Note that this is a different top-level command (s3api) than the one we used to create the bucket. You can see what the full command looks like here:

```
$ aws s3api put-bucket-acl \
    --bucket learnjs-logging.benrady.com \
    --grant-write URI=http://acs.amazonaws.com/groups/s3/LogDelivery \
    --grant-read-acp URI=http://acs.amazonaws.com/groups/s3/LogDelivery
```

Now that it's writable, we need to configure our web-enabled S3 bucket to use this new bucket as a target for logging requests. So now is the time to use the s3api put-bucket-logging command.

S3 groups like Log Delivery are not the same thing as IAM groups.

Rather than passing in all the options for this command on the command line, we're going to use the --cli-input-json option and control the configuration with an external .json file. This is the same approach we've used in the previous chapters with the sspa script, so we'll use the same directory to store this configuration: the conf directory.

You can create a sample configuration for this command by using the --generate-cli-skeleton option. Run these commands to create the configuration file in the conf/s3 directory:

```
$ aws s3api put-bucket-logging \
--generate-cli-skeleton > conf/s3/«your.bucket.name»/logging.json
```

Open the file you generated and take a look. Fill in (or remove) these values:

learnjs/8000/conf/s3/learnjs.benrady.com/logging.json

```
{
    "Bucket": "",
    "BucketLoggingStatus": {
        "LoggingEnabled": {
            "TargetBucket": "",
            "TargetGrants": [
                {
                    "Grantee": {
                        "DisplayName": "",
                        "EmailAddress": "",
                        "ID": "",
                        "Type": "",
                        "URI": ""
                    },
                    "Permission": ""
                }
            ],
            "TargetPrefix": ""
        }
    },
    "ContentMD5": ""
}
```

The top-level fields are options to the put-bucket-logging[5] command. Start by filling the Bucket field with the name of our S3 web bucket. The BucketLoggingStatus

---

object controls where the logs are written and who can access them. The ContentMD5 field is just a signature for the request, which you can remove.

Inside the LoggingEnabled object, there are three fields. TargetBucket is the name of the logging bucket, which you should fill in. TargetPrefix lets you specify a subdirectory in the target bucket to use when writing the logs. If you want to reuse a logging bucket across many different apps, this can be useful.

The TargetGrants field can be used to grant access to a user or group. However, in our case, we want the TargetGrants section to be empty. This is because S3 is one of Amazon's oldest services, and it's not as integrated with the IAM service as other services. In addition to access granted by IAM, S3 has its own security model...one that we don't need to use. So after making all these changes, you should wind up with a configuration file that looks like this:

learnjs/8010/conf/s3/learnjs.benrady.com/logging.json

```
{
    "Bucket": "learnjs.benrady.com",
    "BucketLoggingStatus": {
        "LoggingEnabled": {
            "TargetBucket": "learnjs-logging.benrady.com",
            "TargetGrants": [],
            "TargetPrefix": ""
        }
    }
}
```

Now run this command to configure logging for our web bucket:

```
$ aws --profile admin s3api put-bucket-logging \
    --cli-input-json "file://conf/s3/learnjs.benrady.com/logging.json"
```

S3 access logs are delivered in batches. It can take up to a few hours for the logs of a request to be delivered to the bucket. Amazon also makes no guarantee about these being complete,[6] calling it a "best effort" system. Since we're going to be aggregating the data in these logs anyway, that's not a problem.

Analyzing S3 Logs

Now that we're capturing logs in S3, how do we look at them? As our app grows, we'll need powerful tools to analyze the millions of requests it handles. There's going to be too much data to read the logs to know what's going on. We'll have to a find way to aggregate the data to see the complete picture.

---

6.   https://docs.aws.amazon.com/AmazonS3/latest/dev/ServerLogs.html#LogDeliveryBestEffort

Thankfully, to do this with AWS S3 access logs, you don't need expensive, dedicated systems for log analysis; you can use the tools right in front of you. Using the same s3 sync command we use to deploy our website, we can quickly download the log files we've collected for our app. Once we've got them downloaded, we can use some simple (but powerful) command-line tools to analyze them. When used effectively, these tools are fast and can easily consume gigabytes of log data in the blink of an eye. To download the logs from your logging bucket into a logs directory, run these commands:

```
$ mkdir logs
$ aws s3 sync s3://learnjs-logging.benrady.com/ logs
```

Because S3 logs are delivered in batches, the individual log files will never be updated. This is nice, because the s3 sync command will only download the files you don't have stored locally. So as our application gets more and more traffic, the log files will get bigger, but you won't be stuck downloading them over and over again to stay up to date. Using *nix command-line tools and column-oriented log files, you can quickly extract useful information from large datasets. While you may already be comfortable doing this kind of analysis with these tools, let's take a quick look at how you can use them on the log format that S3 gives us.

If you open up one of these log files, you'll see long lines with a lot of columns, each representing different attributes of the request. Here's an example of a log for a single request, with each space-delimited column on a separate line:

```
1c6655153443675143ce57960dd49971b0745bdd3175be16afd5229a33ded86f
learnjs.benrady.com
[13/Jan/2016:04:30:48
+0000]
98.223.150.212
1c6655153443675143ce57960dd49971b0745bdd3175be16afd5229a33ded86f
42AFE21FCF9C87AA
REST.GET.LOGGING_STATUS
-
"GET
/learnjs.benrady.com?logging
HTTP/1.1"
200
-
527
-
37
-
-
"-"
"S3Console/0.4"
-
```

The first thing you notice when looking at the logs this way is that some of the data fields are spread over multiple columns. For example, the third field, which is the request time, spans two columns because of the space in between the datetime and the timezone offset. If we collapse this log message down into fields instead of columns, and label them, it becomes a little easier to see what's going on.

```
Bucket Owner: 1c6655153443675143ce57960dd49971b0745bdd3175be16afd5229a33ded86f
Bucket: learnjs.benrady.com
Time: [13/Jan/2016:04:30:48 +0000]
Remote IP: 98.223.150.212
Requester: 1c6655153443675143ce57960dd49971b0745bdd3175be16afd5229a33ded86f
Request ID: 42AFE21FCF9C87AA
Operation: REST.GET.LOGGING_STATUS
Key: -
Request URI: "GET /learnjs.benrady.com?logging HTTP/1.1"
HTTP Status: 200
Error Code: -
Bytes Sent: 527
Object Size: -
Total Time: 37
Turn Around Time: -
Referrer: "-"
User-Agent: "S3Console/0.4"
Version ID: -
```

 Dashes in S3 logs represent data that is not available for that request.

Most *nix command-line tools work effortlessly with line- and column-oriented text. Using tools like uniq and cut, you can quickly and efficiently slice up this kind of data into any form that you want. Let's look at some examples to understand how you can do this, and see what insights we can coax out of these log files.

Bash Pipelines

Bash shells (and other shells like zsh) can easily string together commands using the | operator, known as the *pipe* operator. The pipe operator lets you use the output of one program as the input of another program. You can combine many different programs together to easily create tools to transform, analyze, convert, retrieve, and store data. The combination of these programs, tied together with pipes, is often called a *pipeline*.

Response Code Frequency

To analyze these logs, we're going to create a series of Bash pipelines. We'll use a small set of command-line tools to select the data we want, sort it, and group it for easy analysis.

All these pipelines start with a command to print the contents of our log files. Usually we can use cat, which concatenates the contents of the selected files and prints them out for the rest of the pipeline to consume. If we want to analyze all the files, we simply select them all with *, as you can see here:

```
$ cat logs/* | cut -d ' ' -f 13 | sort | uniq -c
    94 200
     8 304
    20 404
```

The next command in the pipeline is cut, which can easily grab a single column or a set of columns. By default, cut uses the tab character as a delimiter. Using the -d option allows us to specify a different delimiter, the space character. The -f option specifies which column to select. Passing 13 to that option selects the HTTP Status field from the log messages, printing them out one line at a time.

The last thing we want to do is get a count of the occurrence of each distinct status code...a poor man's histogram, of sorts. To do this, we can use the uniq command with the -c option, but uniq requires that its input be sorted, so we use sort to do that.

The inauspicious output of this command tells us everything we need to know. If you're looking for flashy charts and graphics, these aren't the tools for you, but looking at this output tells us that we've had ninety-four HTTP 200 responses, twenty 404 responses, and eight 304 responses...304? Huh. That's interesting...wonder what that could be?[7] Oh, right! 304! The HTTP code that saves you money on data transfer feeds. It's nice that we have some of those, too.

Popular Resources

AWS delivers this log data in batches, each in a different file with a date-time stamp. By using different wildcards for selecting files, you can filter results by time or date. For example, using the square bracket matcher [], you can select a specific subset of files, showing you which resources were requested the most often on January 11th, 12th, and 13th:

---

7.   https://httpstatuses.com/304

```
$ cat logs/2016-01-1[123]* | cut -d ' ' -f 11 | sort | uniq -c| sort -rn
   12 /?location
   11 /vendor.js
   11 /app.js
   10 /images/HeroImage.jpg
    9 /favicon.ico
    9 /
    8 /learnjs.benrady.com?logging
    6 /learnjs.benrady.com?versioning
    4 /learnjs.benrady.com?website
    4 /learnjs.benrady.com?tagging
    4 /learnjs.benrady.com?requestPayment
    4 /learnjs.benrady.com?prefix=&max-keys=100&marker=&del...
    4 /learnjs.benrady.com?policy
    4 /learnjs.benrady.com?location
    4 /learnjs.benrady.com?lifecycle
    4 /learnjs.benrady.com?cors
    4 /learnjs.benrady.com?acl
    4 /?replication
    4 /?notification
    1 /worker.js
    1 /index.html
```

In this case, you can see that a few requests were made to resources that aren't in our app. Perhaps this was a web crawler? Or something more nefarious? Being able to quickly pull data out of our logs with just a few simple commands makes it easy to see these kinds of patterns.

Usage by Time of Day

It can often be helpful to get a sense of *when* people are using your app. If you capacity plan for 10,000 new users over the course of a day, but they all tend to show up between 5 p.m. and 8 p.m., you're going to have to allocate resources differently than if they were spread out over twenty-four hours. This information is in the logs...you just need to get it out.

To understand what a pipeline is doing, it's often helpful to run it one piece at a time, appending commands at each step, until you can see the final output. If you try it for yourself, you'll probably want to do that with the following pipeline (which was long enough that it didn't fit on a single line).

```
$ cat logs/* | awk '{ print $3 }' | tr ':' ' ' | \
    awk '{ print $2 ":" $3}' | sort | uniq -c
   16 04:25
    1 04:27
   30 04:30
   17 04:31
    3 04:32
   25 04:37
```

```
20 04:38
 2 04:46
 8 15:24
```

Here, we're using another command, awk. Awk is a fully fledged programming language, but its ubiquity in *nix environments, support for text processing, and terse language make it a great candidate for processing data in a Bash pipeline. In this example, we're using awk in two places. The first call to awk selects out the date and time portion of the request timestamp. The timezone isn't included in this column, but for what we're trying to do, that's not a problem.

After selecting out the date-time stamp, we use the tr command to replace colons with spaces. We also could have used sed, but tr has a shorter syntax for a simple replace operation like this. Once we've split the date-time into columns, we then send it on to our second use of awk, which reassembles just the hour and minute back into a single string. We then sort this and do a uniq -c to group the data by hour:minute of the day, across all the days in our selected log files.

The log files you get from S3 logging might not be fancy, but when you use a few simple command-line tools, they can tell you amazing things about how, when, and if people are using your applications. Alerting and data collection like this are essential if you want to make improvements to your apps over time. Otherwise, you have no way to know if the changes you made had the intended effect. Now that we can see what the users are doing with our app, it's time to optimize it, which is what we'll do in the next section.

Optimize for Growth

Thanks to the highly scalable services that we use in our application, we can deliver our app to millions of users. In the worst case, we can achieve this by just spending more money...but by optimizing both our single page app and the services that it uses, we can get more out of each dollar that we spend. In addition, certain characteristics of our app can't be improved by just giving Amazon more of our money. These characteristics, like the application load time, require understanding and action on our part in order to change.

Caching for Lower Cost and Load Time

In the web analytics world, the term *bounce rate* describes the percentage of users who request your web page or app but never interact with it. It's kind of like a customer who walks into a store, doesn't like what they see, and turns around and walks out. Waiting a long time for a page to load is one thing that can cause users to bounce from a site.

Since we're building a single page app, it has a huge advantage over a traditional web app in that it only has to load once—but it still has to load before anyone can use it. To ensure we don't keep users waiting, we need to ensure it loads in a just a few seconds. Getting the load time and application size as low as possible will ensure the app is available to the widest possible group of users.

Before we can start optimizing our application-loading process, we need to understand what our app is doing right now. To do that, we can use the built-in development tools in your favorite browser. We'll use Google Chrome for this example, but you can get similar functionality from other browsers such as Firefox and Internet Explorer. When you open the Chrome Developer Tools, you should see a toolbar that looks like this:

Click the Network tab, and browse to the application's production URL (not localhost). This tab shows you all the network requests the browser makes on behalf of our application.

From this, we can see our application is making more than a dozen requests for a total of 405KB of data. Probably more than you expected, right? The good news is that by adding metadata to the items in our S3 bucket, we can include a *Cache-Control* header on these responses, causing subsequent requests to be fetched from the cache instead of over the Internet to our S3 bucket or CloudFront edge location.

Cache-Control headers in S3 are controlled using metadata applied to each item in the bucket. By default, these headers are not added. By using the -I option in curl, you can do a HEAD request to see what headers are currently present on a particular resource:

The Cache-Control Header

One of the great things about building apps on top of established protocols like HTTP is that solutions often exist to problems that you run into. If the cliché about hard problems in computer science is right, cache invalidation on the web is one of those things you really don't want to have to fix by yourself. Thankfully, this problem is often solved through the use of the *Cache-Control* header.[a]

Browsers use this header to determine when they need to go back to the server to get a fresh copy of a particular resource. Web servers and proxies, in turn, can use it to determine when their copy of a resource is out of date. Setting this header on the responses from your web host will let you control how your application is loaded, and it lets you greatly reduce the time and bandwidth needed to load your app.

---

a. https://developers.google.com/web/fundamentals/performance/optimizing-content-efficiency/http-caching?hl=en

```
$ curl -I http://«S3_Bucket_Endpoint»/vendor.js
HTTP/1.1 200 OK
x-amz-id-2: «id_tag»
x-amz-request-id: B3FCCF13142A9CCD
Date: Wed, 20 Jan 2016 18:43:30 GMT
Last-Modified: Tue, 05 Jan 2016 02:36:22 GMT
ETag: "210f8bac1f6ada8d5ecf9ca74e176a6b"
Content-Type: application/javascript
Content-Length: 193464
Server: AmazonS3
```

So right now, none of the resources in our app are served with a Cache-Control header. We should add them, but carefully. We have two kinds of resources, and they each need their own cache policy. For infrequently changing resources, like our vendor.js file and hero image, we want very aggressive caching. Once users download these resources, it's unlikely they'll ever need to download them again. Telling the browser to keep the resources in the cache saves money on S3 data-transfer costs and makes the app load faster.

For frequently changing resources, like the index.html and app.js, we want the browser to check for new versions every time the apps loads. This allows S3 to either return an HTTP 304 (as we saw earlier) if the resource is unchanged, or send the updated version. Caching these frequently changing resources can cause the app to break in unexpected ways if the cache for one resource is updated, but not another. For example, an update to the JavaScript that references a template that isn't in the cached HTML will cause the app to break.

Preventing these resources from being cached also makes our S3 logging more useful. It means that whenever a user attempts to load our app, those resources will show up in the logs. Doing a count of the requests for those resources then becomes a reliable measure of how often our app is loaded.

To add the metadata for the Cache-Control header, you can use the AWS CLI command s3api put-object. This is a more fine-grained version of s3 sync, the operation used by the sspa script to deploy our app. You'll want to specify a max-age value in this header to set the length of time the resource should be cached (in seconds). You can run this command on each resource you want to cache, as you can see in the example here:

```
learnjs $ aws s3api put-object \
  --profile admin \
  --acl 'public-read' \
  --bucket learnjs.benrady.com \
  --cache-control 'max-age=31536000' \
  --key vendor.js \
  --body public/vendor.js
```

Now, when fetching this resource, S3 includes the Cache-Control header with the values we specified.

```
$ curl -I \
  http://learnjs.benrady.com.s3-website-us-east-1.amazonaws.com/vendor.js
HTTP/1.1 200 OK
x-amz-id-2: «id_tag»
x-amz-request-id: 7EB6F7458CC636C9
Date: Wed, 20 Jan 2016 18:44:08 GMT
Cache-Control: max-age=31536000
Last-Modified: Wed, 20 Jan 2016 18:43:47 GMT
ETag: "210f8bac1f6ada8d5ecf9ca74e176a6b"
Content-Type: binary/octet-stream
Content-Length: 193464
Server: AmazonS3
```

Now this resource will be cached for 31,536,000 seconds—also known as 365 days. This metadata will persist, even if you use the sspa script to deploy the app again.

Invalidating Caches with Versioned Filenames

You might be wondering what happens when we change a file with a one-year cache age. Changing a file like vendor.js without forcing the cache to update would likely cause errors in our app. A simple approach to solving this problem is to stop using the cached resource...just give it a different name!

By appending a version number, tag, or digest on the end of any resource you change, you can easily update resources with long cache lifetimes. Referencing these new versions in index.html means that when the browser goes to fetch them, it won't have a cached version of that resource, since the name will be slightly different. It will then go all the way back to our S3 bucket and fetch the most recent version.

When you rename something like this, remember to update any references to it in both the index.html and tests/index.html files. Otherwise, your tests will start failing.

Applying these techniques, you should be able to cache most of the resources in the application. Once you've applied the appropriate metadata to the items in the S3 bucket, turn off the Disable Cache button in your browser development console. Load the app twice (by hitting Enter in the address bar), and you'll be able to see what requests a typical user would make when loading the app for a second time. It should look something like this:

With the cache enabled, our app only checks the index.html and app.js files, loading all the remaining resources from the cache. This greatly decreases our load times (from 441ms to 324ms, in this example) and data transfer rates, creating a better experience for the user, and lower costs for us.

 Most browsers will ignore cache headers when you hit either Ctrl-R or F5.

Costs of the Cloud

For applications that have a handful of users, the cost of a serverless application usually rounds down to free. Amazon offers most of its services at no cost,[8] as long as you stay under a set limit of resource use. The incremental

---

8.   http://aws.amazon.com/free/

costs of usage above this free tier are often extremely low. Even for moderately sized applications, the costs of exceeding these limits can be just pennies per month. This can be an advantage over solutions like virtual server hosts, which charge a fixed cost per month whether you have one user or ten thousand.

However, while the initial costs of cloud services can be extremely low, they often increase with each user of your system. If you're not careful, these costs can add up quickly. With all this auto-scaling wizardry at your fingertips, how do you know you won't wind up with a huge bill at the end of the month if your application suddenly gets popular?

The first step in avoiding this problem is understanding what your costs per user would actually be. You can reasonably estimate this cost, based on the pricing and capacity information provided by Amazon. By contrast, in order to accurately measure the capacity (and price) of a traditional web app, you'd probably have to build a prototype and load test it to see how much traffic it could handle. The fact that we can reasonably estimate the cost of using cloud services to support a given number of users, before building a system, is another amazing benefit of a serverless approach.

To estimate the costs for our app, we need to make some educated guesses about how users will use it. Let's walk through all the services we use, and try to figure out how much it will all cost.

Loading Costs

When our application is first loaded, it is served out of S3. S3 acts merely as a web server and plays no part once the app starts. S3 charges us for storing this data, responding to the request, and transferring it. If you look back at the performance analysis we just did, you'll see that the first time our app is loaded, it makes four requests to S3, for a total size of 261.5KB.

Because of the caching we added, subsequent loads only consume a few hundred bytes and a couple of requests. So as we add new users, we'll generally only have to pay the costs of them loading the app for the first time. We can calculate these initial loading costs using the pricing information provided by Amazon. Here are the prices for S3 services in the us-east-1 region as of January 2016:

Storage cost	Request cost (GET)	Transfer cost
$0.03/GB	$0.004/10K requests	$0.09/GB

This means the loading cost of our app, including request and transfer fees, will be $0.24 for every 10,000 users. Subsequent requests to validate cached items in S3 would cost less than 1/100th of that. The storage cost of hosting our app in S3 is negligible (less than a penny a month) and would not increase as we add users.

Data Costs

Once the app is loaded, some users will want to save their answers. To do that, they'll need to connect using Cognito. For our purposes, Cognito is a free service. Costs are associated with Cognito Sync—a feature designed to synchronize data between clients—but we're not using that in our app.

Using the security credentials obtained from Cognito, the app will make direct requests to DynamoDB to save and fetch the user's data. Like S3, Amazon charges for data transfer out of DynamoDB, but as we saw in Chapter 5, *Storing Data in DynamoDB*, on page 93, it also charges for read and write capacity. Since we purchase this capacity ahead of time, this gives us an easy way to control our spending with this service.

As with most things on the web, only a fraction of our users will likely want to connect and save their answers. If we assume a fairly conservative rate of five percent, we can estimate the necessary capacity and cost of DynamoDB. Here are Amazon's prices for DynamoDB services (as of January 2016):

10 write capacity units	50 read capacity units	Transfer cost (out)	Transfer cost (in)	Storage cost (after 25GB)
$0.0065/hour	$0.0065/hour	$0.090/GB	Free	$0.25/GB/month

With our assumed conversion rate, we would expect 500 users out of every 10,000 to connect and save answers in our app. If we have one hundred questions in our app, and conservatively estimate that users will answer all of them, then for every 10,000 users, we'll need the capacity to perform 50,000 writes over the lifetime of the account, which isn't much. To put this in perspective, the AWS Free Tier for DynamoDB lets us perform up to 2.1 million writes *per day* at no cost.

Because a serverless app only uses the services it needs, we can keep our data costs low. Unlike an app based on a middle-tier application server that stores session information in a database, our app only accesses the database when absolutely necessary. As your applications grow, you can provision read and write capacity units whenever you want, and release them when you don't need them, paying by the hour. Once you determine how much capacity your apps need for typical usage, you can buy reserved capacity in one- or three-year terms by paying an up-front cost to get lower costs per hour.

Microservice Costs

As we just saw, understanding the pricing model of a service lets us design for low cost. To best integrate the microservice we created in Chapter 6, *Building (Micro)Services with Lambda*, on page 113, we need to accommodate the constraints and capabilities of Amazon Lambda. Then we can tailor our app to strike the right balance of performance and cost.

As we've already seen, Amazon charges for Lambda services by the gigabyte-second. The more memory and time our function takes to run, the more we pay. We also pay per request, although the cost is quite low at $0.20 per million requests (and the first million per month are free). We set the size and duration limits of our service at 512MB over five seconds, so given those limits, we can calculate the maximum total cost of running our service for a fixed number of requests.

As of January 2016, Amazon lists the price[9] of a 512MB Lambda function execution at $0.000000834 per 100ms, or $0.0000417 for five seconds. Lambda charges in 100ms increments, so the chances of a successful execution costing that much are low, but that's the maximum. That means 10,000 executions of our service would, in the worst case, cost $0.417. Additionally, the Amazon Free Tier provides for 400,000 gigabyte-seconds of execution at no cost. While this means our microservices will have to get very popular before they starting costing money, this cost doesn't include the additional DynamoDB read capacity we'd need to buy to support this service, which would vary based on the amount of data we have. So is there something we can do to reduce the cost of this service?

The first thing we might want to do is tune the resource limits to fit the actual needs of the function. Five seconds was a guess, and might be more than this function ever really needs. That is, if it's running for that long, there's probably something wrong, and there's no sense in spending money on a request that's going to fail anyway. We might also be able to reduce the memory size with a smarter service implementation. The first version of our service was fairly naive, and using some of the paging features of DynamoDB might be a way to keep the memory footprint small as the number of users grows.

---

9.   https://aws.amazon.com/lambda/pricing/

To reduce our read capacity needs, we could require that users authenticate before using this service. If the features that it supports are compelling, this will simultaneously drive up our conversion rate and keep the costs of supporting this service down by limiting the number of requests. Of course, whether or not this is appropriate for this application (or any other) depends on the goals of the app, but saving the more expensive services for premium users can sometimes be the easiest way to keep costs down.

Adding It Up

So let's say we add 85,000 new users a month, and our app hits just over one million users in the first year. To support these users, we'll buy twenty-five additional write and read capacity units to augment the twenty-five units we get in the Amazon Free Tier. Based on our previous calculations, this is well above what we would expect the number of writes to be over the course of a year, but we have to account for spikes in traffic.

 Buying capacity based on *average* usage means your app will be broken half of the time.

Next, we need to pay for the transfer costs to DynamoDB. Amazon charges the same amount for this data transfer as it does for S3, which is $0.09 per gigabyte. However, we only have to pay for the outgoing data. Data sent to DynamoDB is free. The answer records in our app are small (under 1KB), so even with each of our connected users answering one hundred questions each, our data transfer costs will be almost negligible.

For our microservice, let's say we limit usage to connected users, and that a typical connected user will access that service ten times in a year. This means that in the first year, we would expect to have 500,000 invocations of our Lambda service. Since the first million requests per month are included in the Free Tier, and this service is well below the Free Tier limit for execution costs, we won't have to pay anything to support our first million users. Lastly, since we're using Cognito and external identity providers to manage user accounts, we don't have any costs there.

Putting all these costs and estimates together, we can project how much money our app will cost if one million people load our app in the first year. The total cost, as you can see in the table here, works out to about $195, or $0.54 a day.

Service	Capacity	Cost
Static web hosting	1 million application loads	$23.64
Identity management	50,000 user profiles	Free
Write capacity	1.5 billion writes (max)	$142.35
Write data transfer	5 million 1KB writes (average)	Free
Read capacity	1.5 billion reads (max)	$28.47
Read data transfer	5 million 1KB reads (average)	$0.43
Microservices	500,000 executions	Free

Of course, this is just an estimate, and our actual costs would depend on how people actually use the app, but these are promising numbers. We know that even with millions of users, our costs per month will be manageable. And because we don't have to host an application server tier, we're saving the cost of virtual or physical servers, which not only cost money to run (whether anyone uses them or not), but also can take more and more time to administer as we scale them horizontally.

Scaling up an application is never easy, but now that you understand the technology, the tools, and the costs, maybe you'll feel ready to build a serverless app. As demand increases, your assumptions about how people will actually use your app will be tested, and you may be surprised by what your users do. Sometimes the surprises are pleasant, and sometimes...not so much. But building a serverless application gives you a lot of flexibility to respond to challenges quickly and effectively. You can turn the knobs up to eleven to handle unexpected demand, and literally buy time while you adapt. Or you can turn things down to save money when usage patterns change. With a serverless app, you can switch between those two extremes at a moment's notice.

Deploy Again (and Again, and Again...)

There are two kinds of software: the kind that changes, and the kind that dies. If your apps are useful and successful, you will have demands to change them...to add new features, support more users, and store more data. The ability to squeeze additional value out of already existing code is one of the most valuable skills a developer can have. If you're good at it, you can do it indefinitely.

The approach you've seen in this book will help you do this. As your applications grow and change, the tests we added will help you deploy over and over again with confidence, knowing that the functionality you added a day, a month, or a year ago is still working. The simple tools we used to build our app will remain practically relevant for years to come, and the infrastructure we used can accommodate new users and features while keeping costs low.

Now that you've mastered the tools and techniques in this book, here are some additional topics you might want to investigate.

Next Steps

Can I Reuse This Workspace?

Yes, you can reuse the prepared workspace for your own projects if you wish. Unlike the content in this book, the workspace is available under the MIT license. However, you may need to make changes to the sspa script to accommodate your apps.

Creating a Client Logging Web Service

By creating a Lambda web service that uses the CloudWatch API, you can write log messages directly from the web app. Attaching a handler to window.onerror[10] allows you to capture any JavaScript errors and send them to CloudWatch for later analysis. You can even create alerts, as we did earlier in this chapter, to let you know when your users are experiencing problems.

Keep in mind that you cannot trust the log messages that you get from the browser when performing security audits. Messages may be fabricated, or simply absent, because attackers (and everyone else) have complete control over what happens in their browser. However, these logs can be useful when troubleshooting legitimate problems.

Going Global with CloudFront

As we saw in the last chapter, serving our application out of Amazon's CloudFront is a great way to fend off denial-of-service attacks. CloudFront also provides a caching mechanism that's more sophisticated[11] than what S3 provides. As your users spread across the globe, you might want to look at some of the ways CloudFront can reduce your costs and improve the experience users have with your apps.

---

10. https://developer.mozilla.org/en-US/docs/Web/API/GlobalEventHandlers/onerror

11. http://docs.aws.amazon.com/AmazonCloudFront/latest/DeveloperGuide/Expiration.html

Installing Node.js

Amazon Lambda runs Node.js v4.3.2, which you can download from node-js.org.[1] Whatever method you use to install it, you'll want to get as close to that version as possible.

Installing the Node.js Runtime

Depending your operating system, you can use one of the following methods.

Linux

One of the great things about working with open source software in a *nix environment is that you can always build your tools from the original source code. Node.js is no different. Follow the download link at the start of the appendix, and choose either the 32-bit or 64-bit tarball (depending on your OS). Then download, unzip, and follow the instructions in the README file.

If you don't want to build Node.js from source, you have some other options. If you're using Ubuntu or another Debian-based distribution, you can install Node.js with apt, but there are a few caveats. First, the exact version of Node.js that Lambda uses may not be available. At the time of this writing, the latest version you can get through the public repositories is v0.10.25, which is significantly different from the Lambda version.

Another issue with installing the Debian packages is that the name of the binary is different than the source install. Rather than the command name node, the Debian package installs the Node.js interpreter as nodejs. This can create problems for node packages (like Jasmine) that depend on the node binary being available via the path.

---

1.   https://nodejs.org/download/release/v4.3.2/

If you do install Node.js via the Debian package, you'll need to correct this problem. You can create a symlink in the /usr/bin directory that has the correct name. Run these commands, and you should be all set:

```
$ cd /usr/bin
$ sudo ln -s nodejs node
```

You can also install Node.js via yum on Red Hat or CentOS, but at the time of this writing, those versions were even further from the Lambda Node.js version (v0.12+), so I don't recommend it.

OS X

If you're working on OS X, you can download a binary Node.js installer from the download link at the start of this appendix. Just unpack it and follow the instructions. This is the most straightforward way to get the specific version that Lambda uses.

You can also install Node.js via Homebrew and MacPorts, but the version you get may not be the same as the Lambda environment. Use this with caution.

Windows

Just as with OS X, downloading the Node.js binary is a straightforward way to get the exact version running on Lambda. Follow the download link at the start of the appendix, then step through the Windows installation wizard.

Managing Multiple Node.js Versions

What if you already have Node.js installed, but not the right version? It's possible to install and use multiple versions of Node.js with a tool called *nvm*.[2]

Using the nvm command, you can switch between different versions of Node.js, and even install them, with a single command. To install the version of Node.js that Lambda uses, you can run this command:

```
$ nvm install v4.3.2
```

And to use it, you can run this:

```
$ nvm use v4.3.2
```

You can have multiple versions installed at the same time, in case you're working with different environments (a combination of Lambda and EC2, for example), or if you want to use a different version of Node.js for local tools than you do for testing Lambda functions.

---

2.   https://github.com/creationix/nvm

Assigning a Domain Name

The S3 endpoint URLs aren't really intended for human consumption, so if you're using them to access your application, you'll want to get a better domain name if you intend to share this application with other people. Thankfully, S3 lets you easily associate a domain name with your bucket using a *CNAME record*.

Your domain registrar should provide instructions about how to create CNAME entries for a domain name. You'll want to create one for the domain that shares a name with our S3 bucket. Just be sure to enter the *endpoint* (not the bucket name) as the value for the CNAME entry. The endpoint URL contains the bucket name and the availability region where it's hosted, like this:

```
learnjs.benrady.com.s3-website-us-east-1.amazonaws.com
```

You can map an S3 endpoint like this to the domain or subdomain that matches the bucket name. If configured to serve static web content, the S3 bucket will handle requests to this endpoint just as if they had been sent to your original hostname.

Once the CNAME entry has been created, you can use the dig command to check and make sure it's right, even before the changes have replicated to other DNS servers. You just need to know the nameserver of your registrar. For example, here's how I checked my DNS entry:

```
$ dig @ns1.hover.com learnjs.benrady.com +short
learnjs.benrady.com.s3-website-us-east-1.amazonaws.com.
```

Note the dot on the end of the CNAME entry. That's required by DNS. If your registrar didn't add that for you, you may have to edit the entry to add it yourself. Once this DNS change propagates, you should be able to see the app in any browser.

Creating DNS Records

DNS stands for Domain Name System, and it's how your computer translates the hostname of a URL into an IP address that it can actually connect to. DNS is used for all kinds of protocols on the Internet, including HTTP, FTP, SSH, and email protocols like SMTP and IMAP. There are different kinds of DNS records, and the one you need depends on what you're trying to do. Often, domains will have a *A record* that points to an IP address on the Internet. Since Amazon S3 may change the IP address of a bucket at any time, you can't rely on that IP address to create an A record. For this app, you want to create a CNAME record, which maps a domain name to another domain name.

Each DNS entry also has a time to live, or TTL, which determines how often it refreshes the record from your registrar's name server. This can range from one minute to one day, so it may take some time for changes to your DNS entries to propagate through the network of DNS servers. Until these changes propagate, you won't be able to browse to your app. You can try to speed up the process by clearing your system's DNS cache.

Bibliography

[Hav14]   Marijn Haverbeke. *Eloquent JavaScript: A Modern Introduction to Program-ming.* No Starch Press, San Francisco, CA, second, 2014.

[How14]   Shay Howe. *Learn to Code HTML and CSS: Develop and Style Websites.* New Riders Press, Upper Saddle River, NJ, 2014.

Index

The Modern Web

Get up to speed on the latest JavaScript techniques.

Deliver Audacious Web Apps with Ember 2

It's time for web development to be fun again, time to write engaging and attractive apps – fast – in this brisk tutorial. Build a complete user interface in a few lines of code, create reusable web components, access RESTful services and cache the results for performance, and use JavaScript modules to bring abstraction to your code. Find out how you can get your crucial app infrastructure up and running quickly, so you can spend your time on the stuff great apps are made of: features.

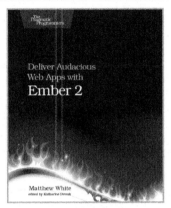

Matthew White
(154 pages) ISBN: 9781680500783. $24
https://pragprog.com/book/mwjsember

Reactive Programming with RxJS

Reactive programming is revolutionary. It makes asynchronous programming clean, intuitive, and robust. Use the RxJS library to write complex programs in a simple way, unifying asynchronous mechanisms such as callbacks and promises into a powerful data type: the Observable. Learn to think about your programs as streams of data that you can transform by expressing *what* should happen, instead of having to painstakingly program *how* it should happen. Manage real-world concurrency and write complex flows of events in your applications with ease.

Sergi Mansilla
(142 pages) ISBN: 9781680501292. $18
https://pragprog.com/book/smreactjs

Secure and Better JavaScript

Secure your Node applications and make writing JavaScript easier and more productive.

Secure Your Node.js Web Application

Cyber-criminals have your web applications in their crosshairs. They search for and exploit common security mistakes in your web application to steal user data. Learn how you can secure your Node.js applications, database and web server to avoid these security holes. Discover the primary attack vectors against web applications, and implement security best practices and effective countermeasures. Coding securely will make you a stronger web developer and analyst, and you'll protect your users.

Karl Düüna
(230 pages) ISBN: 9781680500851. $36
https://pragprog.com/book/kdnodesec

CoffeeScript

Over the last five years, CoffeeScript has taken the web development world by storm. With the humble motto "It's just JavaScript," CoffeeScript provides all the power of the JavaScript language in a friendly and elegant package. This extensively revised and updated new edition includes an all-new project to demonstrate CoffeeScript in action, both in the browser and on a Node.js server. There's no faster way to learn to write a modern web application.

Trevor Burnham
(124 pages) ISBN: 9781941222263. $29
https://pragprog.com/book/tbcoffee2

Put the "Fun" in Functional

Elixir 1.2 puts the "fun" back into functional programming, on top of the robust, battle-tested, industrial-strength environment of Erlang. Add in the unparalleled beauty and ease of the Phoenix web framework, and enjoy the web again!

Programming Elixir 1.2

You want to explore functional programming, but are put off by the academic feel (tell me about monads just one more time). You know you need concurrent applications, but also know these are almost impossible to get right. Meet Elixir, a functional, concurrent language built on the rock-solid Erlang VM. Elixir's pragmatic syntax and built-in support for metaprogramming will make you productive and keep you interested for the long haul. This book is *the* introduction to Elixir for experienced programmers.

Maybe you need something that's closer to Ruby, but with a battle-proven environment that's unrivaled for massive scalability, concurrency, distribution, and fault tolerance. Maybe the time is right for the Next Big Thing. Maybe it's *Elixir.*

This edition of the book has been updated to cover Elixir 1.2, including the new with expression, the exrm release manager, and the removal of deprecated types.

Dave Thomas
(354 pages) ISBN: 9781680501667. $38
https://pragprog.com/book/elixir12

Programming Phoenix

Don't accept the compromise between fast and beautiful: you can have it all. Phoenix creator Chris McCord, Elixir creator José Valim, and award-winning author Bruce Tate walk you through building an application that's fast and reliable. At every step, you'll learn from the Phoenix creators not just what to do, but why. Packed with insider insights, this definitive guide will be your constant companion in your journey from Phoenix novice to expert, as you build the next generation of web applications.

Chris McCord, Bruce Tate, and José Valim
(298 pages) ISBN: 9781680501452. $34
https://pragprog.com/book/phoenix

Seven in Seven

From Web Frameworks to Concurrency Models, see what the rest of the world is doing with this introduction to seven different approaches.

Seven Web Frameworks in Seven Weeks

Whether you need a new tool or just inspiration, *Seven Web Frameworks in Seven Weeks* explores modern options, giving you a taste of each with ideas that will help you create better apps. You'll see frameworks that leverage modern programming languages, employ unique architectures, live client-side instead of server-side, or embrace type systems. You'll see everything from familiar Ruby and JavaScript to the more exotic Erlang, Haskell, and Clojure.

Jack Moffitt, Fred Daoud
(302 pages) ISBN: 9781937785635. $38
https://pragprog.com/book/7web

Seven Concurrency Models in Seven Weeks

Your software needs to leverage multiple cores, handle thousands of users and terabytes of data, and continue working in the face of both hardware and software failure. Concurrency and parallelism are the keys, and *Seven Concurrency Models in Seven Weeks* equips you for this new world. See how emerging technologies such as actors and functional programming address issues with traditional threads and locks development. Learn how to exploit the parallelism in your computer's GPU and leverage clusters of machines with MapReduce and Stream Processing. And do it all with the confidence that comes from using tools that help you write crystal clear, high-quality code.

Paul Butcher
(296 pages) ISBN: 9781937785659. $38
https://pragprog.com/book/pb7con

Long Live the Command Line!

Use tmux and Vim for incredible mouse-free productivity.

tmux

Your mouse is slowing you down. The time you spend context switching between your editor and your consoles eats away at your productivity. Take control of your environment with tmux, a terminal multiplexer that you can tailor to your workflow. Learn how to customize, script, and leverage tmux's unique abilities and keep your fingers on your keyboard's home row.

Brian P. Hogan
(88 pages) ISBN: 9781934356968. $16.25
https://pragprog.com/book/bhtmux

Practical Vim, Second Edition

Vim is a fast and efficient text editor that will make you a faster and more efficient developer. It's available on almost every OS, and if you master the techniques in this book, you'll never need another text editor. In more than 120 Vim tips, you'll quickly learn the editor's core functionality and tackle your trickiest editing and writing tasks. This beloved bestseller has been revised and updated to Vim 7.4 and includes three brand-new tips and five fully revised tips.

Drew Neil
(354 pages) ISBN: 9781680501278. $29
https://pragprog.com/book/dnvim2

The Pragmatic Bookshelf

The Pragmatic Bookshelf features books written by developers for developers. The titles continue the well-known Pragmatic Programmer style and continue to garner awards and rave reviews. As development gets more and more difficult, the Pragmatic Programmers will be there with more titles and products to help you stay on top of your game.

Visit Us Online

This Book's Home Page
https://pragprog.com/book/brapps
Source code from this book, errata, and other resources. Come give us feedback, too!

Register for Updates
https://pragprog.com/updates
Be notified when updates and new books become available.

Join the Community
https://pragprog.com/community
Read our weblogs, join our online discussions, participate in our mailing list, interact with our wiki, and benefit from the experience of other Pragmatic Programmers.

New and Noteworthy
https://pragprog.com/news
Check out the latest pragmatic developments, new titles and other offerings.

Save on the eBook

Save on the eBook versions of this title. Owning the paper version of this book entitles you to purchase the electronic versions at a terrific discount.

PDFs are great for carrying around on your laptop—they are hyperlinked, have color, and are fully searchable. Most titles are also available for the iPhone and iPod touch, Amazon Kindle, and other popular e-book readers.

Buy now at *https://pragprog.com/coupon*

Contact Us

Online Orders:	*https://pragprog.com/catalog*
Customer Service:	*support@pragprog.com*
International Rights:	*translations@pragprog.com*
Academic Use:	*academic@pragprog.com*
Write for Us:	*http://write-for-us.pragprog.com*
Or Call:	+1 800-699-7764